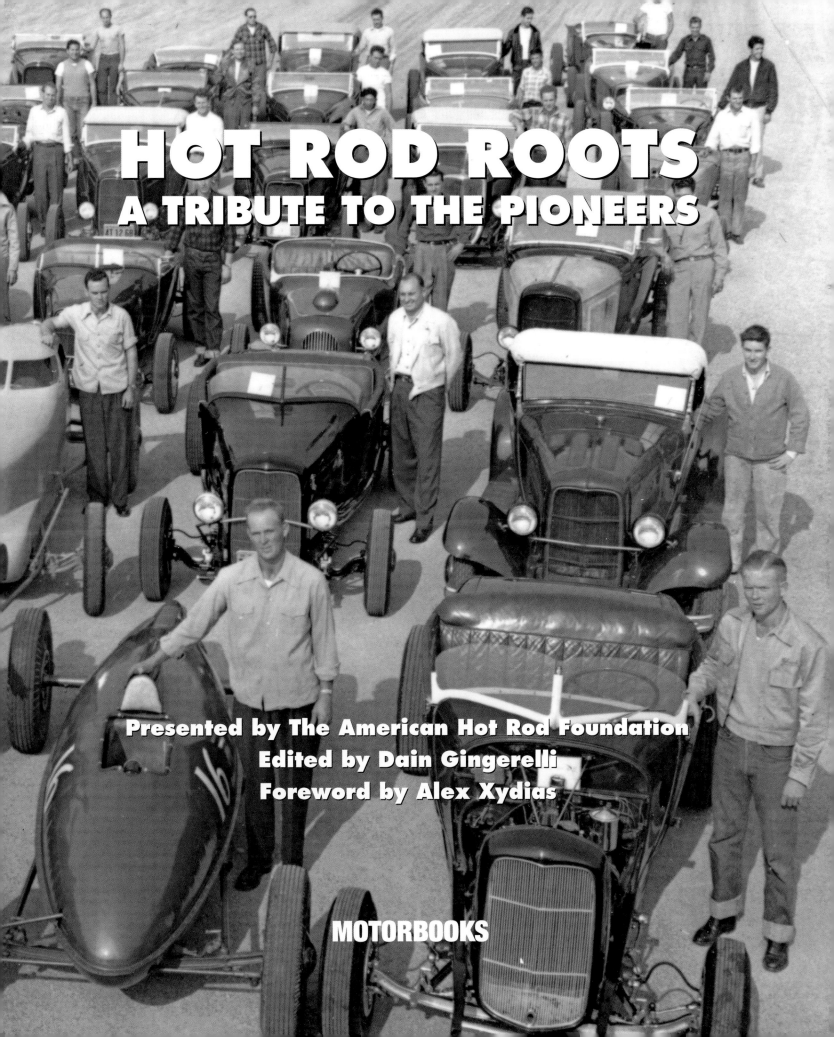

HOT ROD ROOTS
A TRIBUTE TO THE PIONEERS

Presented by The American Hot Rod Foundation
Edited by Dain Gingerelli
Foreword by Alex Xydias

MOTORBOOKS

First published in 2007 by Motorbooks, an imprint of MBI Publishing Company, Galtier Plaza, Suite 200, 380 Jackson Street, St. Paul, MN 55101 USA

Motorbooks titles are also available at discounts in bulk quantity for industrial or sales-promotional use. For details write to Special Sales Manager at MBI Publishing Company, Galtier Plaza, Suite 200, 380 Jackson Street, St. Paul, MN 55101 USA

Library of Congress Cataloging-in-Publication Data

Hot rod roots : a tribute to the pioneers / Dain Gingerelli, editor.
    p. cm.
  Includes index.
  ISBN 978-0-7603-2818-7 (hardbound w/ jacket)
1. Hot rods—United States—History. I. Gingerelli, Dain, 1949-
TL236.3.H6835 2007
629.228'60973—dc22
                            2007021844

Acquisitions and Project Editor: Dennis Pernu
Designer: Jennifer Maass

Front cover: A former U.S. Marine and one of the country's premiere custom auto upholsterers, Tony Nancy first made his mark with this blown flathead-powered '29 Model A highboy that recorded a best of 138 miles per hour in Modified Roadster. Tony followed up with a fuel-injected Buick Nailhead–powered '29 that ran a best of 10.54 at 134 miles per hour. *Tony Nancy Collection/Courtesy Petersen Publishing Company*

Frontispiece: Before Christmas tree starting lights were planted at NHRA-sanctioned strips across the country, racers relied on flag starters. New England's two most famous flag-wavers were "Air" Leo Errara (shown) and "Flying" Dick Zaido. Both men helped flag at the Orange drag strip. *Xenophon Beake*

Title pages: This overhead shot of cars belonging to SCTA members was taken to help promote the Hot Rod Expo in 1948. This show, held at the Los Angeles Armory, became even more famous as the birthplace for *Hot Rod* magazine. *Robert E. Petersen Collection*

Back cover: The second time out for Marvin Lee's Class B Streamliner netted a top speed of 146.81 miles per hour, good for first in class. Wayne Horning built its 1942 248-cubic-inch Chevy six-cylinder engine. Horning used a cylinder head and intake manifold of his own design, and mounted a Spalding ignition and Scintilla magneto. *Ian Dunn Collection*

Printed in Hong Kong

CONTENTS

Foreword
By Alex Xydias

Shortly after World War II ended, many returning servicemen—including me—had a lot of catching up to do in life. We pursued our dreams with a gusto that is hard to describe today. My dream was to open a hot rod speed shop, which I did in the city of Burbank, California.

But on one particular Monday I had a problem. I was out of money! Well, actually, *I* wasn't out of money; there was probably 20 bucks in the cash box under the counter. It was the So-Cal Speed Shop's advertising budget that was out of money. Wally had come in and pressured me into buying a quarter-page ad in the SCTA Racing Program for $10. Selling ads was one of the many jobs he did as the unofficial general manager of the Southern California Timing Association. He was the SCTA's first full-time employee and we really needed him to help cope with the huge growth we had following the war.

Anyhow, the following morning, Tuesday, Pete stops by to sell me an ad in his new car magazine. Not only was the So-Cal ad budget kaput, I wasn't sure that Pete's magazine would be successful so I told him no!

I've made many mistakes in my lifetime, but that ranks right near the top. Of course, the magazine did OK—well, better than OK—and I advertised in *Hot Rod* for many years. I had originally met Pete a few months earlier when he was part of a group working with Wally and the SCTA to produce the Hot Rod Exposition at the National Guard Armory in Los Angeles. Among other things, Pete served as the group's photographer. He was 20 years old.

On Wednesday of that same week I had to go over the hill to Hollywood to pick up two sets of heads and a dual-carb manifold at Vic's shop. I would also pick up some business advice, because by now Vic had become my mentor and we would work closely together for many years.

If you've been able to follow all of this, you will have some idea about how wonderful and simple it was in those early days. Please note: In three days I spent time with Wally Parks, Robert E. "Pete" Petersen, and Vic Edelbrock Sr.—three men who would become icons in our hobby, our sport, and our industry! And that was only part of it—on Thursday, I went to Phil Weiand's for some manifolds, and to Ed Winfield's for some cams.

When Pete passed away in early 2007 I realized how important it is to remember and document those early days of our history, and what an incredible job The American Hot Rod Foundation is doing in that regard. This book is an excellent example of their efforts. I know you will enjoy it.

It's 1954, and Alex is ready to make a pass in the '34 Ford that *Hot Rod* magazine dubbed the *Double-Threat Coupe.* Courtesy Alex Xydias

Introduction

By Steve Memishian, Founder, The American Hot Rod Foundation

In the fall of 2002, I had been a hot rodder for less than 10 years. I was curled up in my family room, eagerly rereading Dean Batchelor's wonderful book, *The American Hot Rod*, for the third time and babbling interesting snippets to my tolerant wife, Carol. At some point she asked me if any of these pioneers of hot rodding whom Dean was writing about were still alive. In a few days, we had the answer that perhaps half of them were not only alive and well, but in many cases still building and racing cars. This was the answer Carol wanted, along with the stunning information that less than a handful of them had ever been recorded on film or tape. An emotional Italian with a huge heart and a passion for collecting historical objects, Carol quickly convinced me that making video oral histories of these special men that Dean had known was worth whatever the cost might be.

With those marching orders, I turned to Ed Almquist's *Hot Rod Pioneers* and, with help from my friend Dave Crouse, began making a list of all the contributors still talking and walking Fords and flatheads. A few weeks later, I contacted a friend of mine, Henry Astor, to see if he might conduct the first few oral histories as a test-bed. Henry had produced two excellent television documentaries and I guessed he could be lured away from the advertising research business. That done, we rang up the first few pioneers, and the rest is history.

We were incredibly well received by these gracious men, few of whom had ever been confronted by a professional television crew and all of the lighting equipment, cameras, audio gear, and excitement involved. And here I had thought we would be turned down, or made to wait, or booked and canceled. But every gentleman showed up on time and answered Henry's many questions with poise and an enthusiasm that told me they realized they would now be made a permanent, living part of hot rod history. Four years later, our vault now contains well over 300 hours of network-quality tape from interviews with more than 160 pioneers. And our historian, Jim Miller, continues to research and caption more than 20,000 wonderful vintage photos given to us by the pioneers. We have achieved Carol's simple goal. The challenge now is to create documentaries and books that can make The American Hot Rod Foundation a financially viable entity in the years to come.

Early on in this great adventure, I began assembling an advisory board of experts who knew far more about the history and culture of hot rodding than did I. These very special people—Ray Brown, Steve Coonan, Dave Crouse, Robert Genat, Ken Gross, Debbie Lewis, Phil Linhares, Mark Morton, Greg Sharp, Jim Stroupe, and Alex Xydias—have helped me and the foundation in countless ways. Now, as a special treat for you, our reader, four noted authors from this group have written on favorite topics for this historically important book, supplemented by chapters from our wonderful editor, Dain Gingerelli (who also provided captions), the prolific Pat Ganahl, and from the Northeast, Mr. A. B. Shuman.

Enjoy, and please visit us at www.ahrf.com!

CHAPTER 1

World War II and Battle of the Bulge veteran Ak Miller resumed his dry lakes racing after the war. Here he steers a semi-streamlined '27 Model T down the Bonneville Salt Flats. Miller's accomplishments behind the wheel stretched into a variety of racing categories. *Robert E. Petersen Collection*

WORLD WAR II & HOT RODDING

Think of the postwar rodder as "G.I. Go"

By Robert Genat

DECEMBER 7, 1941, was like no other day in the lives of the men and women who would later become known as the Greatest Generation. Thousands of Americans had been killed after a sneak attack on U.S. military forces stationed at Pearl Harbor, Hawaii, by Japan's naval air force. This attack galvanized the American population and, within days, the United States declared war on Japan.

America already had been gearing up for possible participation in the war because of the attacks on our ally, Great Britain. For more than a year the United States' great industrial might had been providing Britain with airplanes, ships, and other weapons and technology needed to defend itself against Germany. By the time America entered the global conflict, California's aircraft industry was on point, building and developing new fighter and bomber aircraft for the Allies.

Manning the machines and aircraft assembly lines at the manufacturing plants of North American, Boeing, Lockheed, and Douglas were young men whose technical ability in the aircraft industry came, in part, from their experience building hot rods during their carefree days before the war. The innovative spirit that, before the war, had created hot rods would be seen throughout the war. Reciprocally, the lessons learned and the machinery created *during* the war would be directly translated back into the hot rod world during the ensuing peacetime.

In the immediate days following the Japanese attack on Pearl Harbor, the lines of young men wanting to enlist in the U.S. military overwhelmed recruiting stations. Many potential enlistees were given deferments from military service because of their work in defense plants. Simply put, their work producing war matériel was too important to overlook.

But many of those young men simply wanted to be a part of the action and walked away from their safe, high-paying jobs to serve their country and be part of the adventure overseas. Young men like Jack Calori, a hardcore hot rodder and dry lakes racer, could have easily dodged military service and made a lot of money building airplanes in the safety and warmth of Southern California's Douglas Aviation factory. But Calori was determined to become a sailor and work on U.S. Navy airplanes. Part of his motivation to join the navy stemmed from a poster he saw as he walked into the Douglas plant one day. The poster featured sailors and marines. "I thought it would be great to get into the navy and to get aboard the aircraft carrier *Enterprise*," recalls Calori. "I told Douglas I was quitting and they said, 'You can't quit—your job is essential, it's wartime, you have to stay here and work.' Later I went down to the navy recruiter and they wouldn't take me—same story about my job being essential."

Calori was advised to make a demand on the company for more money and a different job on the day shift, and if they didn't meet it, they had to let him join the navy. So Calori created his list of demands, asking to be put on the day shift working on the A-20 Havoc bomber line. His demands

(Opposite page) Outrider club member Gus Rollins sits in the Rollins-Nelson entry at Harper Dry Lake. The Model A roadster, powered by a Ford flathead V-8, ran 89.91 miles per hour on this particular day, August 18, 1940. *Taylor Family Collection*

(Below) Frankie Lyons ran a four-port Riley with two carburetors in his modified. The car, sporting number 24 at this June 25, 1933, meet, turned 112.50 miles per hour. Early hot rods like this were often referred to as "gow jobs." *Nordskog Family Collection*

Pete Clark, owner of Uptown Garage at 10th and Western in Los Angeles, ran this 1923 T body with '27 Whippet grille on a Model A frame at Muroc Dry Lake. The car competed in Class F where it ran 111.80 miles per hour on April 30, 1933. Muroc Dry Lake later became Rogers Dry Lake, the focal point for Edwards Air Force Base. *Nordskog Family Collection*

also included a ten-cent-per-hour raise. Calori's demands were met. But he was determined to join the navy and went back to the recruiter. When the recruiter asked if he was employed, Calori lied. He was sworn in and could finally leave Douglas Aircraft Company to work on navy planes.

Wally Parks, instrumental in founding the National Hot Rod Association (NHRA) after the war, also had a deferment because of his job as a tank test driver at the General Motors Tank Assembly Plant. Like so many others, he didn't want to miss this once-in-a-lifetime adventure, so he enlisted. Because of Parks' experience with tanks, he was sent to the Aberdeen Proving Ground where the army tested tanks and trained tank crews. Later, his overseas assignment also involved tanks. "I shipped overseas to the South Pacific and joined a tank battalion's maintenance division in Guadalcanal," says Parks. "It turned out to be the only army tank battalion in the South Pacific." Parks also saw duty in Bougainville, Luzon, and Leyte Gulf.

Then, as now, dry lakes racers didn't compete for money. However, every competitor was issued a timing tag indicating his best run. This one shows that Gus Rollins' roadster went 103.80 miles per hour at Muroc Dry Lake during the September 28, 1941, meet. *Jack Underwood Collection*

THIS CERTIFIES THAT

CAR NUMBER 348

THIS MEYER V8

OWNED BY GUS ROLLINS HAS TRAVELED

AN ELEC. TIMED 1·4 MI. IN 8.67 SEC. OR 103.80 M.P.H.

COURSE MUROC DATE 9·28·41

SOUTHERN CALIFORNIA TIMING ASSOCIATION, INC.

Like Calori, Jim Nelson—after the war a member of the Carlsbad (California) Oilers Club, a lakes racer, a drag racing chassis builder for Dragmaster, and 1962 Winternationals Top Eliminator winner—wanted to join the navy, but various physical problems prevented him from serving. "I wanted to go in so damn bad just for the experience of it," says Nelson. "I tried to join the navy and they wouldn't take me because I was deaf in one ear and I also had a hernia in one side." Nelson took a bus up to Los Angeles to an induction center for a pre-induction physical. The overworked military doctors who preformed Nelson's physical didn't notice that when they gave him the hearing test he really didn't plug his good ear, or that the cough for the hernia test was more of a throat clearing. Nelson passed the physical and was sworn in and sent directly to the navy's boot camp a few miles south in San Diego.

Lakes racer and So-Cal Speed Shop founder Alex Xydias also had a job that qualified him for a military deferment. "I wanted to go in as an airplane mechanic and work on fighter planes and bombers," says Xydias. "What hot rodder wouldn't want to do that?" So Xydias volunteered to join the U.S. Army Air Corps. They gave him a test to gauge his mechanical aptitude, and following boot camp Xydias was sent to Luke Field in Arizona where he worked on AT-6 trainers. He eventually worked on P-40 fighters and B-25 bombers before being trained as an engineer/gunner for B-29 bombers.

Most hot rodders entered the military with a fundamental set of mechanical skills, having used only the most basic of hand tools. They may have known how to weld, but many had never used an arc welder. They may have had only adjustable or a few open-end wrenches. Those lucky enough to have worked in machine shops before entering the service would learn to appreciate the exceptional quality of the milling machines and lathes that the government bought for their use. Now, through the war effort, hot rodders who had been getting by with minimal equipment had the best that taxpayer money could buy.

Along with high-quality machine tools, the government offered excellent training. The young recruits were taught the right way to build, repair, and service machinery. Those working on electronics were taught that just twisting two wires wasn't good enough—the connection had to be soldered. Young men working on aircraft structure learned how to repair a combat-damaged tail or wing so the aircraft would be safe for another flight. Men who had hastily bolted together a flathead engine back home learned that the high-quality fasteners on aircraft engines were also safety-wired to prevent them from backing out in the middle of a dogfight. Before the war, slapdash work on an old roadster was acceptable. If the car's engine or transmission quit, the driver could just coast to the side of the road. But sending a Corsair or Hellcat into air combat meant that everything had to be done right. Engine failure in a dogfight at 8,000 feet and 75 miles from the carrier was not acceptable to the navy or to the pilot flying the plane.

The hot rodders who remained at their defense jobs found that life at home during the war was full of shortages and sacrifices. They worked long hours to keep the troops overseas supplied with weapons and matériel. Many hobbies and pastimes, including auto racing, were put on hold for the duration of the war. Indeed, gasoline and tires were strictly rationed, prompting many young men to put their roadsters up on blocks. They relied on public transportation and car-pooling, and some rodders bought old motorcycles to ride to work. The industries that made hop-up parts before Pearl Harbor now used their machinery to produce war goods. Hot rodding was put on hold indefinitely until the Axis Powers were defeated. Occasionally, late at night after the second shift ended, a couple of roadsters might drag race on a desolate boulevard somewhere in Southern California.

Even though the war brought hot rodding to a near standstill, the enduring passion for the sport was not forgotten. Guys overseas still talked about it with other men in their outfits. (These young enthusiasts came from all over America, too.) Hot rodders also demonstrated that anything could be made functional with the kind of ingenuity used on their own cars back home. "During World War II, it was proven that it was an advantage to have mechanical skills," recalls Parks. "We got way high on the mountains in Luzon and the tanks lost their horsepower. As an experiment, I found out that by taking a radiator drain cock and plugging it into the intake manifold, I could allow more air in and all of a sudden the thing ran up the hill." Parks also installed a Ford V8-60 into a Jeep while overseas.

Other mechanics also figured out all too soon that Ford's small, 60-horsepower flathead would fit into the Jeep's tiny engine compartment. Tom Medley, stationed in Germany during the occupation after the war, was one of them. "I was driving a Jeep all the time in an infantry outfit," says Medley.

This 1941 article in *Colliers* magazine didn't overlook the hot rodding–military connection. It read in part: "Today you will find [the hot rod builder] and an endless stream from the same mold, pouring into sprawling aircraft factories, well-equipped for his task in defense industries. At aviation schools he is being turned out as the master mechanic . . . creator of horsepower."

"It was stock, but ran pretty good. I was coming down the Autobahn one day and an air corps Jeep with dual pipes went by me like I was chained down. And he was pulling a trailer! I said, 'There goes a California car. I'll bet you a dollar they've got a V8-60 in that thing.'"

Then, as now, anyone serving in the military loves to receive letters from home. During World War II letters often were exchanged between servicemen in different theaters. One of the best pieces of mail any hot rodder got during the war was Veda Orr's *SCTA News* (often referred to as *CT News*). Orr, the wife of speed-shop owner Karl Orr and a prominent lakes racer herself, created *CT News* to keep dry lakes racers in contact with each other and with their friends back home. She sent it to rodders stationed overseas and to those who remained stateside working in the defense industry. Since there was no racing at the time, her newsletter consisted of news from soldiers and sailors all over the world. "That was the glue that kept the guys together," recalls Jim Nelson. "It was the communication link between guys who may have been in the Philippines, England, or Texas." Veda Orr's *CT News* kept the hot rod embers burning, and is one of reasons why dry lakes racing resumed so quickly after the war.

When American soldiers and sailors returned home after the war, they left behind countries in ruin and many dead comrades. Those who survived the fighting returned to their own communities. They wanted to buy homes and raise families. Some resumed their old jobs or went to school, while others formed their own businesses. They rarely discussed their experiences, and when pressed, downplayed their roles overseas.

(Above left) They weren't fancy, but the early issues of *SCTA News* helped define what dry lakes racing was all about. They also listed event speeds and records, and gave updates about club members and their cars. All for a nickel!

(Above right) Although racing was suspended through the duration of World War II, Veda Orr continued to publish the *SCTA News*, which served as a message board and newsletter for the racers serving in the U.S. military at all points around the globe.

Many people consider Veda Orr to be the First Lady of Automobile Racing. She competed and set a speed record in her roadster built by her husband, Karl Orr, who also raced modifieds during that time. Both were members of the Albata car club.

Most servicemen who served overseas had left their hot rods in garages or up on blocks. They hoped to find them there upon their return. However, family members often sold hot rods for badly needed cash, or stripped them of parts to keep other cars running. Sadly, other hot rods simply disappeared or were stolen.

Not every hot rodder returned home to find things just as they had been upon their departure. In 1940, Japanese-American dry lakes racer Frank Morimoto volunteered for the national draft, a program that required only one year of military service. Shortly before his term of enlistment was to expire, Japan attacked Pearl Harbor. Morimoto was sent to the army's 442 Regimental Combat Team, an all-Japanese-American unit. By the end of the war, the 442nd had fought with distinction in North Africa and Europe, and was among the most decorated units in the war. Members of the 442nd were awarded 21 Congressional Medals of Honor, 4,000 Bronze Stars, and 9,486 Purple Hearts. "We were a specialized group of only one regiment, which is only one-third of a division," says Morimoto. "I was proud to be a member of that organization."

While Morimoto fought in one of the most heralded units in the U.S. Army, his parents were sent to an internment camp in Wyoming. Even when he returned home on leave to Southern California, he was treated poorly because of the racial hysteria that gripped the nation after Pearl Harbor. Another dry lakes racer, Keith Landrigan recalls, "I was told that when he [Morimoto] came home on leave, the army sent guards with him for his own protection." Sadly, when Morimoto returned to his home after the war, his car and all his racing gear were gone. He ultimately found certain components in various speed shops, but he decided to give up hot rods. "That was the deciding factor in my leaving hot rodding," says Morimoto. "I was a married man with a young child, and the wife said, 'No more hot rodding.'"

Events worked out differently for Xydias. While serving in the air corps, he dreamed of starting a speed shop after the war. He loved the sound of the phrase "speed shop," as in "Karl

Orr's Speed Shop," and he wanted to build one in Burbank, California. It took the army two months to process his paperwork and in that time he was able to locate a building, finish the inside, and stock its shelves with a few parts. "I wasn't selling a lot of expensive items at first," says Xydias. "I sold a lot of steel wheels. The guys were going from the Kelsey-Hayes wire wheels to steel wheels. I was

A typical scene at the local speed shop or auto garage might witness some young men—who probably gained a little more knowledge about mechanical things during their military service—taking a cigarette break.

good friends with the Ford dealer in the area and they would call me when they'd get a shipment of steel wheels in and I'd buy every one of them." Xydias also had a full stock of trim rings and hubcaps to complement the new wheels. "I also sold a lot of Stewart Warner gauges and chrome acorn head nuts." He was smart enough to know that right after the war the hot rodders were concerned first with getting their cars running and looking good. A need for speed would come later.

Xydias and many other speed shop owners also stocked surplus military goods on their shelves. The military bought the best of everything and bought a lot of it. When the war ended, much of that same equipment—surplus now—went for pennies on the dollar. "The first [seat]belts we had were military surplus," says Dick Flint. "I used to go to a surplus house in Los Angeles where they had huge bins of surplus items—they were at least 10-foot square and filled with seatbelts." Flint used to climb inside, pair up the best sets, and throw them over the side. Other favorite surplus items for lakes racers were aviator goggles and cloth flying helmets. Surplus aluminum bucket seats from fighters also found their way into dry lakes roadsters.

Servicemen returning from the war brought a few more speed secrets with them, among them streamlining methods. The result, as seen here, was a more eclectic gathering of cars on the dry lake beds during SCTA meets.

One of the best surplus bargains and slickest items for the dry lakes were belly tanks that could be turned into streamliners. Belly tanks, also known as drop tanks, were auxiliary fuel tanks attached to the underside of an aircraft's wings or on the centerline to extend the range of the aircraft. The term *drop tank* refers to the pilot's ability to drop the tank for improved aerodynamics in case of a dogfight. The idea of turning the ubiquitous aircraft belly tank into a racer came to Bill Burke while he was gazing at a barge full of belly tanks. "I got to looking at them and I thought, 'Holy Toledo, that looks like it would make a wonderful streamliner,'" says Burke. "I went over on the barge and they let me measure the tank. I was sure then that it would be ideal for the dry lakes."

Following the war, the government released thousands of these expendable tanks as surplus goods. They came in two basic sizes: a smaller tank used on Mustangs, Thunderbolts, and Corsairs; and a larger tank used on P-38s. While some were made out of paper (totally disposable without the use of critical materials), most were made from aluminum or steel. Farmers loved the larger ones—they cut them in half and used them as watering troughs for cattle and livestock.

Following the war, Burke found a surplus yard on Alameda Street in Los Angeles that had wing tanks. "I went there immediately," recalls Burke. "The owner had a smaller wing tank from a P-51. That was the first wing tank I built. It was so small that it was really unsafe—it was ridiculous." Burke's first tank featured a solidly mounted rear end with the driveshaft running right through the middle. "There wasn't any room for a bucket seat of any kind," says Burke. "So, I welded a bicycle seat on that driveshaft housing." Problem solved, for the time being.

The Burke-Francisco belly tank, here at the 1949 Hot Rod Expo, was virtually unbeatable in 1948. After setting the class record in 1947 at 139.21 miles per hour, the following year it pushed the record to 149.40 and was fastest car at the lakes, running 153.32 miles per hour. It was points champion in 1949. Bill Burke got his inspiration to build the belly tank racer when he was stationed in the South Pacific during World War II. *Mario Baffico Collection*

Burke was onto something but had to refine his idea to enable the driver to sit in the tank. The solution was to use the bigger P-38 tank. He also moved the engine to the rear, leaving the front available for the driver to sit, albeit cramped, well within the confines of the tank's aerodynamic shell. Burke's first of the larger tanks was powered by a stock Don Francisco–built Ford Model A engine. It ran 131 miles per hour. Burke and Francisco later teamed up on Francisco's *Sweet Sixteen* tank. Burke also built Alex Xydias' now-famous So-Cal Speed Shop belly tank.

Bill Burke's creation of the belly tank lakester (as they were called) was typical of the 1940s-era hot rodder. In those days, hot rods were built with ingenuity and basic, seat-of-the-pants engineering. For the most part, creating something from someone's castoff goods was learned during the Great Depression and refined by those who had to make the most of what they were given during the war.

In addition to seatbelts and fasteners, there was an abundance of high-quality surplus sheet aluminum available in the Los Angeles area. "All around Southern California were all these scrap yards, where you could buy surplus military equipment and surplus aircraft," says Lynn Wineland. "We haunted those places. If you wanted a T-6, you could find it—dirt-cheap. We bought it by the pound; it was wonderful!"

Marvin Lee's Chevy-powered Class B Streamliner, shown here at El Mirage Dry Lake on September 25–26, 1948, used the front section of a drop tank for its bodywork. The car ran 146.81 miles per hour for first in class. *Ian Dunn Collection*

Jim Khougaz used the skills he acquired while working on aircraft to build the pan for the underside of his famous '32 Ford roadster. He bought a sheet of 4x10-foot aluminum from a surplus yard to form the pan. "I ran the car without a belly pan for a couple of years, but I finally realized that a belly pan would help—and it did," recalls Khougaz. His work area was the gravel backyard of his father's house. "I started trimming and finally got it," says Khougaz. "It was all handwork, cutting and trimming to fit and making the dimples for the

Eddie Miller used steel tubing to build this chassis for his radical new lakes machine. The car remained on the jack stands in his backyard when this photo was taken, August 29, 1948. *Jim Miller Collection*

differential." Khougaz didn't have an elaborate set of tools to work with, just a couple of pairs of shears and a ball-peen hammer, but he had a wealth of metal-forming knowledge and skills.

Before joining the navy, Don Ferrerg worked at Douglas Aircraft on SBD dive-bombers. His experience taught him how to form sheet aluminum and how to rivet panels. After the war he went back to Douglas, where they had him riveting panels on the Black Widow bomber. "I went back about a month after the war, and I didn't really want to work inside," says Ferrerg. "Working just as a riveter was kind of boring." So he left Douglas to work in an auto body shop where he put his navy metalworking skills to use. "I learned how to build a hood—you know, pound the blisters in it, and rivet it together."

More sophisticated metalworking skills would soon be seen at Southern California Timing Association (SCTA) meets on El Mirage Dry Lake. Before the war, leather straps secured a hood to the car; after the war, sleek, handmade aluminum hoods were locked in place with hidden, trick latches or Dzus fasteners. These and other surplus parts were fitted to vintage Fords by skilled tradesmen.

World War II was certainly a defining moment for a generation of young men and women who experienced that global conflict. They were ordinary people who, through their patriotism and wholesome values, performed extraordinary feats to win the war. After the war, they returned home to resume their lives as ordinary citizens. But those involved in auto racing were quick to incorporate many of the technical skills they had learned into the design

Kenz & Leslie set the Class D Streamliner record of 221.479 miles per hour at Bonneville in 1951. The black lines on the aluminum panels are pieces of yarn taped on to help show airflow at speed over the aerodynamic body during a run. *Ernie Pereira Collection*

In 1951, Bill Burke and Jim and Tommy Dahm ran this Class B Modified Coupe—a chopped Austin/American Bantam body with a Douglas A-26 Invader wing duct modified for the radiator opening—at Bonneville. The car ran 141.509 miles per hour. *Ernie Pereira Collection*

The Chapkie brothers of the Glendale Headers ran this chopped-and-channeled Model A sedan at Bonneville in 1952. It flashed through at a credible 142.80 miles per hour. The streamlined nose section helped its aerodynamics. *Mario Baffico Collection*

of their race cars, making them safer and faster. Those young men came back as more mature and more disciplined car builders. Their talents were put to use by veterans in the business world, too. The military, by its nature, forces people to work together for a common goal. For hot rodders, this level of teamwork could be seen in the SCTA's club network and in the organization of speed trials on the dry lakes.

Indeed, hot rodding and hot rodders benefited from the war in many ways. The same technology used to mass-produce war goods was quickly applied to producing consumer goods. This included a variety of high-quality intake manifold castings and innovative cylinder heads for their hot rods. Moreover, drag racing's transition from street racing to track racing in the late 1940s can be directly attributed to the number of abandoned airfields that dotted California and the rest of the country. These spacious airfields offered the perfect venues for this new form of motorsport.

Today, Americans across the country thank that generation for the sacrifices made during World War II. And we appreciate the ways in which the war effort indirectly and unexpectedly contributed to the ongoing evolution of auto racing, in general, and hot rodding, in particular. Never before had so much been learned by so many in such a short period of time.

CHAPTER 2

The Brissette Brothers–Summers entry at Bonneville in 1960 with Bob "Butch" Summers at the wheel. After qualifying at 264.70 miles per hour, he set a new Class A Lakester record of 251.309 miles per hour. The tank was powered by a supercharged Chrysler Hemi. A few years later, Bob set the land-speed record in the *Goldenrod*, a car built by him and his brother Bill. *Fred and Mary Lou Larsen Collection*

BELLY TANKS

Drop tanks raise the bar for speed

By Pat Ganahl

MANY SAY THAT IT WAS WALLY PARKS who gave hot rodding the tagline "Ingenuity in Action." One of the most graphic examples of this description is the belly tank lakester. If you've never heard this term before, it might sound like something exotic, and in a way it is, coming from aircraft technology. But at the same time it is utterly simple, even pragmatic. That's the way hot rodding can be sometimes.

The belly tank is a perfect example of form following function. But that's starting to sound a bit too academic for us hot rodders. Put in more colloquial terms, it's more akin to "Show us a big, teardrop-shaped aircraft fuel tank—especially one sitting in a surplus pile—and we'll see a ready-made streamliner body."

Belly tankers have appeared in many incarnations over the years. This one, the *No Wash Special* from Tacoma, Washington, was powered by an Evinrude boat motor and appeared at the 1953 Bonneville Nationals. There's no record of its speed. *Julian Doty Collection*

AERODYNAMICS 101

Before we can really understand the bootstrap brilliance of making a streamlined race car out of a teardrop-shaped airplane fuel tank, we have to understand air and the nature of its physics. Not many people do.

A major factor in that lack of understanding is that many hot rodders today were bred on drag racing. Ignoring traction for the moment, if you want to accelerate an object (a vehicle) from a dead stop to a high speed in a short distance, the two primary factors to consider are the amount of driving force required (horsepower) and the vehicle's weight. If you have two vehicles racing from a dead stop to the end of a quarter-mile, there are essentially two things you can do to win: increase horsepower or reduce weight. Most hot rodders tend to think of the former first. Logic says that if you double your horsepower you'll get to the finish line twice as quick. Cut your car's weight in half, and you'll get there twice as quick, too.

But much more pertinent to our current topic—the belly tanker—is a third factor: aerodynamics, or streamlining. We hardly think of it at all because in a quarter-mile sprint it is virtually inconsequential when compared to horsepower and weight.

Even in the early days of hot rodding, as in the embryonic days of the automobile, the true test of speed was flat out—top speed. Sure, early roadster jockeys wanted plenty of "gow" from their stripped-down machines when they took off from a stoplight. But the true test awaited them at the broad, hard, dry lakebeds where you put the pedal down and ran that "job" just as fast as it would go until it "topped out."

So, what made a vehicle top out? Most of today's rodders would shout, "Horsepower!" True, if you add more horsepower the vehicle should go faster. Running a car on the dry lakes is similar to running it on a dynamometer. On a dyno, you run the engine against a load, or a strain, to see how much it pulls before topping out. That point is read as a calculated number, or horsepower. Hop up the engine—make it stronger—and it should pull more load before it tops out, thus making a higher horsepower number. If that engine is in a vehicle racing at the dry lakes or at the Bonneville Salt Flats, that maximum horsepower number will equate to a maximum mile-per-hour number, or top speed. Yes, build more horsepower in the engine and the racer will have a proportionally higher top speed. We're simplifying, of course, but you get the principle. In fact, Bonneville is sometimes called "the great white dyno."

But the question—the point here—is what is the force that holds the vehicle back? What limits it to a given top speed? The answer is air. Oh, a bit of mechanical friction comes into play, but it's not as measurable. Basically, top-speed racing involves pushing air—parting the wind, if you will.

Ermie Immerso's *Valley Auto Special* set fastest speed of the 1956 Bonneville meet at 215.16 miles per hour, with a two-way record of 213.190. The run put Immerso into the Bonneville 200 MPH Club. *Mario Baffico Collection*

Most of us don't think about this because: 1) It's really not a factor in the drag racing that we're more familiar with, or even in blasting around on the street, where we can feel a vehicle's power when we mash the throttle; and 2) We can't see air, and we usually don't notice that we can feel it. We take air for granted. Or, more accurately, we just don't appreciate that it's there.

But the early hop-up artists who tested their cars at Muroc Dry Lake—and even the automotive pioneers who vied for the first land-speed records at places like Ormond Beach in Florida or on frozen lakes in Michigan—understood the significance of streamlining. Some knew this from textbooks, others learned it through experience. Curiously, the shapes of some of the earliest speed-record cars favored the belly tanks we're discussing here.

But let's get back to air. It's definitely *something*. It's made out of molecules, giving it mass. If you don't believe it, watch the wind blow leaves off of trees. That's *something* knocking those leaves off the branches. And when air gets going, it can knock a lot more things down. A gale-force wind, which can tear sails off of ships, is air moving at just 32 to 63 miles per hour. A hurricane, which can uproot trees or knock your house down, is air moving at speeds above 74 miles per hour.

The belly tank racer that Romeo Palimides built for John Olivera as it appeared at Bonneville in 1956. Called the *Romeo Too*, the DeSoto-powered car was clocked at 208 miles per hour, good for second place in Class D Lakester behind Ermie Immerso's *Valley Auto Special* at 213 miles per hour. *Mario Baffico Collection*

The second time out for Marvin Lee's Class B Streamliner netted a top speed of 146.81 miles per hour, good for first in class. Wayne Horning built its 1942 248-cubic-inch Chevy six-cylinder engine. Horning used a cylinder head and intake manifold of his own design, and mounted a Spalding ignition and Scintilla magneto. *Ian Dunn Collection*

When you're driving your car down the road at 74-plus miles per hour through air that isn't moving at all, it's essentially the same as having a hurricane hit your car while it's standing still. Are you getting the picture? Anytime you drive a car on the surface of this planet, you're driving it through air. And air is probably a lot heavier (or "thicker") than you think. At sea level air presses on everything with a "weight" of more than 14 1/2 pounds per square inch of surface. That's a lot. The higher up from sea level you go (or the higher the altitude), the thinner, or "lighter," the air becomes. At that point in our aerodynamics discussion things start getting complicated.

For a better understanding, some people explain aerodynamics by comparing air to water. Water is, of course, much heavier and thicker, but the principles of moving objects through either are similar. Forget the particulars; think of the shapes of fish. Whether by intelligent design or evolution, they're shaped that way because that's what moves through water the easiest, with the least "drag."

Early aerodynamicists studied the shapes of birds but soon focused on raindrops. As it falls through air, a drop of water naturally takes on the teardrop shape we're familiar with. The rounded end forms the front, or leading edge, and the pointy end forms the back. We could get a lot more technical, but this is enough here.

John Vesco owned and built the Vesco-Dinkins entry from San Diego. They fielded this inverted belly tank for many years before turning to streamliners. The car ran 161.00 miles per hour one-way for first in class, and set a two-way record of 156.956 miles per hour at Bonneville in 1953. *Mario Baffico Collection*

Except for two big things.

First is the magnitude of aerodynamics. It's easy to understand that pushing something shaped like a teardrop through the air is a lot easier than pushing something shaped like a brick or barn door. A little more difficult is the concept of "frontal area." This is the size of the object as viewed directly from the front, regardless of its shape. In simpler terms, a teardrop that's twice as big around (viewed head-on) as a smaller counterpart is going to require more horsepower to push through the air than will that smaller counterpart.

But here's the kicker. When we're dealing with weight and horsepower, as in drag racing, things tend to operate in direct proportions. Cut the weight of the car in half, and you'll cut the E.T. about in half. Doubling the horsepower has the same effect. But with aerodynamics things start multiplying exponentially the more air you push. That is, to push your car through the air twice as fast takes four times more horsepower; to go three times faster requires nine times more power. We won't explain it. Just understand that it's a law of physics. A hard law. Fortunately, it works both ways. Decreasing the vehicle's frontal area or improving its aerodynamics by, say, 50 percent will increase your top speed by much more than if you were to increase the engine's power by 50 percent. That's oversimplifying, but you get the

After setting a Class E record in 1954 at 183 miles per hour with two Mercury flatheads, the Hales-Moll team returned the following year as the *Voight Automotive Special*, powered by a pair of Fritz Voight's Chryslers. While their 181 miles per hour speed was first in class, it was shy of their own record. *Mario Baffico Collection*

point: improving aerodynamics is a much more efficient way to increase top speed than simply increasing horsepower.

There's a totally different effect of aerodynamics that is a little harder to explain, but can have disastrous results. It has to do with lift and downforce. Thinner, or lighter, air rises above denser air. As air is heated, it gets thinner (the molecules are spread farther apart) and therefore lighter. That's why a hot air balloon rises in the air. An airplane flies for the same reason, though it's not as obvious. An airplane wing (or "airfoil") is curved on the top surface and flat on the bottom. When the wing moves through the air, the air molecules passing over the curved top surface have farther to go than those passing under the flat, straight bottom.

Ernie McAfee built this car in 1938. It was the first racer to run at Muroc Dry Lake using a tube chassis and streamlined body. McAfee ended the 1938 season as champion, turning a top speed of 137.41 miles per hour at the October 2 SCTA meet. *Howard Humphrey Collection*

Consequently, the air molecules passing over the top of the wing stretch farther apart, creating a vacuum effect that prompts the wing to rise upward.

What's this have to do with dry lakes racers? If you're making a streamlined body for a typical four-wheel vehicle, or even if you're racing a production car (especially those built from the '40s through the present day) at very high speeds, you're pushing something through the air that's shaped a lot like an airfoil: flat on the bottom and curved on the top. At some speeds that thing is going to lift up and fly. And that's exactly what happened to many early streamlined or high-speed vehicles before more was learned about aerodynamic controls. The big wing you see on the back of a Top Fuel dragster today (like wings that have been mounted on all sorts of race cars) is an upside-down airfoil. The curved side is on the bottom, which pulls, or forces, the car down, instead of lifting it up, for improved traction.

EARLY STREAMLINERS

The relevance of this last point to our discussion of belly tanks is that, unlike many of the first land-speed race cars, they don't have a flat bottom and curved top. They weren't made to run on the ground, with four wheels, nor were they made to help lift airplanes into the sky. Simply, a belly tank was an extra appendage on the plane and was designed to cut through the air as efficiently as possible. They offered no additional lift, and in fact were designed to create as little drag as possible. But we're getting ahead of the story here.

One of the earliest and most successful land-speed racers was the Stanley Bros. *Rocket* steam-powered car. It looked surprisingly like the belly tanks we're discussing here, with a thin body tapered at both ends and exposed wheels. It was the first vehicle to travel more than 120 miles per hour, too, doing so in 1906. But it had a rounded top and a flat bottom, its shape

Bob Rufi (wearing the watch cap) took Ernie McAfee's early streamliner concept a step further when he created this slippery little car, the first to break 140 miles per hour at the dry lakes. It was powered by a '25 Chevy four-banger. *Kurt Giovanine Collection*

purportedly based on two previous designs by other racers. The next year, running at an estimated 127 miles per hour, the *Rocket* actually took flight, launching itself for about 100 feet before smashing back to the ground. Some say ripples in the beach surface where it ran caused it to get airborne. Whatever. The point is that 100 years ago they knew that a narrow, tapered, streamlined body was the way to go fast in a vehicle running for top speed on land.

When hot rodders (they weren't called that yet) started racing cars on the dry lakes in the late '20s and '30s, most of the car bodies available were boxy in shape. Notable exceptions were the two Miller racers that Tommy Milton ran during a closed session at Muroc Dry Lake on April 4, 1923, to set some international speed records.

Meanwhile, the local rodders were further spurred by the success of Frank Lockhart's supercharged—and somewhat streamlined—Miller in 1927. They quickly learned that anything they did to make their "rolling bricks" more slippery in the air made them go appreciably faster: smaller, narrower grilles with rounded edges; full, enclosed hoods; smooth covers over spoke wheels, and so on. In fact, some historians feel that Lockhart led the charge by American racers to streamline when he later built his Stutz Blackhawk.

Charles and George Beck purchased Bob Rufi's car after he crashed it. The Beck brothers converted it into an open car and gave it the unique shark's-mouth paint scheme. It's seen headed for Muroc in 1942 where it turned 131.96 miles per hour. Note the resemblance to the postwar belly tank racers. *Jim Miller Collection*

Following his and other racers' examples, it didn't take long for hot rodders to figure out that narrowing the entire car so that it held only one person (effectively reducing its frontal area), made it go *much* faster. In fact, race organizations put these cars in their own class, calling them "modifieds" or "streamliners." In a few years, they found that adding a tapered tail behind the narrowed, truncated roadster body made them even faster, and these became the new streamliners.

Then, a few intrepid, crafty car-builders fashioned their own more-or-less teardrop- or cigar-shaped bodies for their 'liners. Some were pretty crude, as you might expect of home-made bodywork. But they went really fast. Ernie McAfee, for instance, made one that ran 136-plus miles per hour in 1938, but it suspiciously resembled an aerodynamic design used by Mercedes a few years before.

In the years preceding World War II, the streamliner ranks were joined by two buddies, Bob Rufi and Ralph Schenck, who had connections to the burgeoning aircraft industry centered around Burbank, California. They crafted rather sleek, aluminum-skinned streamliners that had enclosed cockpits and ran overhead-valve Chevy four-cylinder engines. With his engine in front, Schenck's resembled Barney Oldfield's successful *Golden Submarine* track racer. Rufi's, with the engine behind the driver, looked very much like the belly tanks that would follow. Further, Rufi enclosed his unsprung rear axle in a fairing and put dished covers on his wheels inside and out. In this form, he ran 143.54 miles per hour in 1940, the first car over 140 and a record that would stand until 1947.

BILL BURKE AND THE BELLY TANKS

Of course a major reason Rufi's record stood so long was because World War II intervened and most of those dry lakes jockeys went off to war. Among them was Bill Burke, an avid, inventive, and resourceful rodder who had built a narrowed T modified to run at Muroc as early as 1937. During the war, while serving in the U.S. Coast Guard, Burke found himself stationed on an island in the South Pacific. One day, while dreaming about what he would build for the lakes when he got home, Burke saw a stack of teardrop-shaped auxiliary airplane fuel

Bill Burke's first belly tank to run at El Mirage wasn't pretty, but it set the stage for a whole new generation of racers at the dry lakes and Bonneville. The car debuted in 1946. With Ed Krogan driving, its fastest speed was 131.96 miles per hour. *Don Ferrara Collection*

tanks on the deck of a ship that had just docked. He knew exactly what he could do with one of them. He went over and measured one and quickly ascertained that a flathead V-8 and early Ford driveline could be squeezed into it.

Unlike smaller, straighter wing tanks that were permanently attached to the wing tips of some later jets, these large, teardrop-shaped belly tanks, or drop tanks, were made in various sizes to fit under the fuselage ("belly") or the wings of fighter planes stationed on carriers and islands. The tanks were designed to significantly increase their flying range. If the plane encountered the enemy, it could drop these tanks to become more maneuverable for combat.

After the war, such tanks (along with all sorts of other war matériel) could be found in surplus yards throughout Southern California for pennies on the dollar. The first one Burke found was a 165-gallon tank from a P-51 Mustang that cost him $35. He cut down a pair of Model T frame rails to fit inside, hung a Model A axle and spring on the front, and dropped a flathead V-8 and driveline behind that. But, like the "guy from Boston with the Austin" in the limerick, there wasn't much room left for the driver. Burke welded a bicycle seat atop the driveshaft tube and built up a small fairing for some protection, but he definitely hung out in the breeze. Still, this less-than-aerodynamic first try with a $35 war-surplus teardrop tank and a mild two-carb '34 Ford V-8 was good for, according to SCTA documentation, 131.00 miles per hour on June 2, 1946. It didn't matter that Burke didn't have the necessary knowledge or talent to hand-form a complicated, streamlined body from flat sheet metal—it was already done . . . for 35 bucks.

The next year Burke found a considerably larger 310-gallon tank from the twin-engine P-38 for his racing. This tank model became the standard for most belly tank lakesters. It was definitely teardrop-shaped, and it was made in two halves that bolted together at a flange around its midsection, making removal of the top half simple for access to the engine or

Another belly tank racer originally built by Bill Burke appeared in 1948 wearing the Lodes Brothers' race livery. It was built from a small 80-gallon tank and later showed up at Bonneville in 1951 with a flame paint job. *Julian Doty Collection*

cockpit. For this tank, on which Burke partnered with engine-builder Don Francisco, he used Model T rails and Model A axles. This time he put the driver in front so that only his head poked out, with a tapered headrest fairing added behind. The engine was placed just ahead of the rear end (using a clutch, but no transmission). A large reservoir between the engine and driver's seat held engine coolant.

This car debuted in 1947, the same year that the SCTA realigned its classes, basing them on engine displacement. Burke's new belly tank racer had immediate success, setting the two-way record for what was still called the Class B Streamliner class. On September 21 of that year, Wally Parks sat in the driver's seat, posting a best-ever run of 139.96 miles per hour. Later that day, Parks drove Burke's tank, dubbed *Sweet 16* for the number it wore, to a blistering 140.84 miles per hour, tops for the meet. By '49, when it was featured on the cover of *Hot Rod*, Burke's car was the first to set a two-way record over 150 miles per hour (at 151.085) and ran an amazing one-way top speed of 164.83. And this was with a relatively small 272-cubic-inch, two-carb Mercury engine burning straight methanol. Clearly, this demonstrates how much more effective streamlining was over making big horsepower.

However, Burke's wasn't the first belly tank to make the cover of *Hot Rod*. Alex Xydias' first So-Cal Speed Shop tank was featured in January 1949. Running in the A Class (smallest engine) with a tiny 156-cubic-inch V8-60, it held that record at just over 130 miles per hour. The car was nearly identical to the Burke-Francisco tank—not surprising, since Burke (called "father of the belly tanks" in the article) helped in its construction.

In fact, during a conversation in 2006 Burke figured he built about 13 belly tanks in those early days. They all used the surplus P-38-type tank halves, the first few having Model T rails, but the later ones using rails made from teardrop-shaped PBY wing struts (also available at the surplus yards). These tanks went to teams such as Breene & Haller and Sanford Bros. &

The So-Cal Speed Shop belly tank lakester was yet to wear its now-famous red and white paint scheme when it first raced April 24, 1948. It was powered by a '39 Ford V8-60 equipped with Edelbrock heads and manifold and a Winfield cam. *Don Ferrara Collection*

Harvey Haller drove the Breene & Haller belly tank at the 1953 Bonneville Nationals in Class D Lakester. The tank ran a 364-cubic-inch Chrysler, qualifying first at 198.76 miles per hour. He later earned a place in the exclusive *Hop Up* magazine Bonneville 200 MPH Club with a two-way average of 209.485 miles per hour. *Mario Baffico Collection*

Phy, but they all looked about the same and all changed ownership (or at least were repainted) several times, making it seem like there were dozens running the lakes and Bonneville through the years. Most estimates put the number of actual belly tanks racing during the '50s and '60s at about 20, maybe even fewer.

The first So-Cal tank was reskinned with a full streamliner body designed by new partner Dean Batchelor, and ultimately ran 210-plus miles per hour before crashing during a meet at Daytona Beach. A second So-Cal belly tank racer, probably the finest of the original breed, was built in 1951 by So-Cal employee Dave DeLangton. Among many new details, he made his own U-channel frame rails from 10-gauge steel and flattened the bottom of the lower tank half to set it closer to the ground. Running nitro-fueled Edelbrock flatheads of various displacements, this car ultimately ran a two-way best of 197.17 miles per hour in '52 at Bonneville, only to be nosed out by Ray Brown's big Chrysler Hemi in Mal Hooper's similar tank at 197.88.

Perhaps the most famous belly tank racer of all time, the So-Cal Speed Shop tank is pushed by the shop truck, a 1940 Ford, on its way to a run down the strip at Bonneville. *Mario Baffico Collection*

Other well-known, record-setting belly tanks of that period included Earl Evans' flamed tank powered by flatheads running his own speed equipment. Charles Scott of Scotty's Muffler in San Bernardino, California, ran a fuel-injected Ardun in his and set a 201.015-mile-per-hour Class B (258-cubic-inch) record at Bonneville in 1953, becoming the first belly tank car to join the exclusive 200MPH Club. Using a quick-change rear end, Scotty ran close to 140 miles per hour with his tank at the Santa Ana Drags. One of the few other tanks to run at the drags was Ray Harrelson's flathead Reco Motor Special in Texas, sometimes piloted by a young A. J. Foyt while vying for Top Eliminator at places like Caddo Mills.

One of the most unusual tankers was that built by ever-creative cam-grinder Howard Johansen. According to the cover story in the December '49 issue of *Hot Rod*, Howard used

two 150-gallon aircraft surplus tanks, lengthening them 4 feet each. The driver sat in the left tank, while the flathead V-8 was placed in the right one, driving a solid rear axle by a chain and sprockets. This twin-tank showed potential but never overcame handling problems that, some say, were attributed to its frame, made of angle iron.

Probably the most beautiful tank ever (though portrayed in an ugly "before" version on a strange February '55 *Hot Rod* cover) was the Art Chrisman–built, purple-and-chrome, Von Dutch–flamed-and-striped, Ardun-powered Reed Bros. Tank. It made the 200MPH Club in 1954 with a 205-plus record at Bonneville. The following year, with John Donaldson at the wheel, the Reed Bros. tank flipped, killing its driver. Donaldson was the first casualty at a Bonneville Nationals event.

Earl Evans was famous for his speed parts. This car, seen here at Bonneville in 1952, used an Evans-equipped 296-cubic-inch Mercury flathead V-8 to set a speed of 183.299 miles per hour and a two-way record of 180.684 miles per hour. *Mario Baffico Collection*

Perhaps one of the most unique belly tank racers was Howard Johansen's twin-tank car. This was his second attempt at mixing two bodies into one car. Sadly, it was as unsuccessful as the first tandem tanker. *Mario Baffico Collection*

A gaggle of fuel lines feed six carburetors atop a Buick V-8 that's neatly tucked into the Johnson & Kimes lakester from Bellflower, California. Running at Bonneville in 1956, the car finished sixth in class with a speed of 193.86 miles per hour. *Mario Baffico Collection*

This shot of Tom Beatty's Class D Lakester shows the intricate space-frame chassis cradling the supercharged 296-cubic-inch Ford flathead. The car set the class record at 203.61 miles per hour in 1952. *Mario Baffico Collection*

Another well-known tank that set many records, ran for many years, and helped pioneer the use of GMC supercharging was Tom Beatty's, which he built himself (including a full space-tube chassis) behind Barney Navarro's shop in Glendale, California. Starting with a 3-71-supercharged 296-cubic-inch Ford flathead in '51, Beatty progressed to 6-71-blown Oldsmobile engines through the early '60s.

By 1962 the latest development in the traditional P-38 tank was the Markley Bros. bright yellow version that mounted the driver, looking through a Plexiglas nose section, completely inside the tank. Behind him sat a small 260-cubic-inch Chevy V-8 with a big GMC blower and Hilborn injector poking into the wind. It ran 239 miles per hour. Also new that year was a longer, cigar-shaped tank (from an F-86 jet) with an injected Chevy small-block in the middle and the driver sitting, slingshot-style, in a formed canopy/tail just behind the rear axle. Both of these cars are still running today, the former in lengthened form by Dennis Varni and the latter in original configuration by the Hammond family.

A few of the other original belly tanks are still around, but you certainly can't buy a new tank for $35 at a surplus yard. Restorers of World War II airplanes have driven the value of

old tanks up exorbitantly. Because of their scarcity, Bonneville racer Jack Kelly of Manhattan Beach, California, recently pulled some molds from the old Scotty's tank to make fiberglass reproductions. The one he currently runs is lengthened 20 inches in the middle for better handling. Recently Rich Venza of Cumberland, Maryland, acquired these molds and offers 'glass tanks in either the original or stretched version through his company, Rod 'n Race.

And enterprising hot rodders are still finding a few new sources of streamlined aircraft tanks to convert into top-speed racers. One hot rodder recently found a 200-gallon wing tank from an F-16 jet, noting that it is designed for supersonic speeds, not just the 400 to 600 miles per hour the old ones were made for. We'll see how fast he goes. And even Bill Burke, who started this whole thing, remains at it. He's not even sure what it came from, but he found a long tank at a good surplus price, built a tube chassis, and stuffed it with an Indy-raced Buick V-6 in time for Bonneville's 50th anniversary meet—which was also *his* 50th anniversary of competing there.

No doubt, belly tanks had a pronounced impact on how racers approached the subject of going fast on the dry lakes and salt flats. And while the cars have changed hands— and changed configurations in the process—one thing remained constant throughout: the racers' accomplishments always came through ingenuity in action, just like it's been since the early days and, chances are, how it will be for years to come.

The Markley Bros. tank as it appeared in 1960. Two years later it was featured on *Hot Rod* magazine's December cover. Dennis Varni owns the tanker today and still runs it at Bonneville, albeit in a much modified condition. *Fred and Mary Lou Larsen Collection*

The early drop-tank lakesters that Bill Burke introduced to dry lakes racing in 1946 inspired other racers to build cars of their own design. This free-form thinking has made land speed record racing very popular among automotive enthusiasts willing to think outside the box.

CHAPTER 3

Del Baxter built this car for the 1947 CRA racing season. He's standing, fourth from left, smiling. By coincidence, the No. 20 car won 20 races that season. A young Troy Ruttman is receiving a trophy for one of his 16 wins in the car. Another future Indy 500 winner, Pat Flaherty, won the other four races. *Don Ferrara Collection*

TRACK ROADSTER RACING

Hot rodding moves forward by going in circles

By Greg Sharp

TRACK ROADSTERS ARE NEARLY FORGOTTEN TODAY, an overlooked chapter in the story of auto racing in America. Although they haven't been raced in anger for a half-century, the "roaring roadsters," as they were often called, played an important role in giving oval-track racing wider popularity among drivers, mechanics, car builders, and fans. Track racers also proved an integral link between professional auto racing and hot rodding. In fact, a large number of early track roadsters saw double duty at the dry lakes and the Bonneville Salt Flats.

According to *The American Heritage Dictionary*, a roadster is "an open automobile having a single seat in the front for two or three people and a rumble seat or luggage compartment in the back." Their simple, sporty style made roadsters popular among performance enthusiasts from the first days of the Model T Ford. Much of the early speed equipment—with names like Frontenac, Winfield, and Rajo—was designed for race cars powered by Model T engines. Much of that same speed equipment was also adapted for street use. By the 1930s, roadsters could be found racing on the dusty, dry lakebeds of Southern California's high desert and on select oval tracks, while impromptu (and illegal) racing also took place on the streets.

Even during the early 1930s, track roadsters were bare-bones cars. This modified roadster had Buffalo-style wire wheels and was powered by a mid-1920s Chevrolet four-cylinder engine. *Nordskog Family Collection*

This Fronty Ford Special in the mid-1930s is seen at Jim Jefferies Ranch in Burbank, California. Burbank Boulevard is just behind the fence. It was common for roadster race cars to wear the word "Special" as part of the team's name on their cowls or tail sections. *Nordskog Family Collection*

Legion Ascot Speedway, at the time located just east of downtown Los Angeles, opened in 1924 and was the showplace of "big car" (not yet known as sprint cars) racing. Fill-in events included roadster races composed mostly of Model Ts, which quickly evolved into fenderless "bobtails," which often had small fuel tanks mounted behind the drivers' compartments.

Among the early race promoters was "Wild Bill" Campbell, who sanctioned a roadster race at the half-mile Riverside Fairgrounds in September 1931. Wild Bill's race was billed as the first race for modified stock cars on the Pacific Coast. Among the most notable roadster races of the '30s was the Gilmore Gold Cup Road Race held February 18, 1934. The Gold Cup took place at Mines Field (the site of today's L.A. International Airport) and was essentially a stock car race consisting of new or nearly new roadsters stripped of fenders and windshields. Of the 27 cars that qualified for the Gold Cup, the vast majority were '32–'34 Fords powered by Henry Ford's new flathead V-8. Stubby Stubblefield collected $1,300 for the win in front of a crowd estimated at 75,000 people.

From the late '30s until the dawn of World War II, modified roadster races consisting of cars with narrowed bodies on shortened frames; hoods, noses, or grilles of the owner's

Say the name *Poison Lil* to any prewar racing buff and they'll mention the names of such drivers as Kelly Petillo, Rex Mays, Stubby Stubblefield, and Mauri Rose. They all drove the car owned by the team of Paul Weirick and Art Sparks. Weirick is seen here in *Lil* as it's ready to be towed away. *Nordskog Family Collection*

Frank McGurk ran this Chevy-powered roadster with a Model T body at Jefferies Ranch in Burbank, California, during the 1930s. Later, McGurk drove the *Abels Auto Ford Special* to 26th place in the 1936 Indianapolis 500. *Nordskog Family Collection*

choosing; and an exposed gas tank positioned behind the driver were run on the half-mile dirt track called Southern Ascot Speedway, located at Atlantic and Tweedy boulevards in South Gate, California.

After hostilities ended in the fall of 1945, hot rodding enjoyed even more popularity than before the war. Today, nonagenarian Wally Parks, among the founders of the NHRA in 1951 and first editor of *Hot Rod* magazine, recalls that the first time he heard the term "hot rod" was from a fellow soldier in the Pacific Theater who hailed from the central California town of San Luis Obispo. Before the war, stripped-down and modified vehicles were known as hop ups or gow jobs (or, less kindly, as jalopies), or they simply were identified by body style (e.g., roadsters, coupes, etc.). The SCTA was formed in late 1937 (Parks was instrumental in its formation, too) and took up where it left off·before the war, running lakes meets beginning in April 1946. The SCTA, which originally allowed only roadsters to compete, was joined by other smaller timing organizations, including the Russetta Timing Association, that accepted enclosed cars such as coupes and sedans. But the monthly trek to the dry lakes that dotted Southern California's high desert was not enough for some speed-hungry kids and veterans. Street racing ran rampant and the "hot rod menace" was the subject of numerous newspaper headlines. Something had to be done.

One outlet was known as the Ash Kan Derby. The Derby was contested on a quarter-mile dirt oval that was graded on Wilson's Ranch on East Third Street in San Bernardino, some 60 miles east of Los Angeles. Would-be racers drove their roadsters to the track, wishfully named Gate City Speedway. Much like at the dry lakes, windshields and headlights were removed and enthusiastic drivers vied for the $25 winner's purse. Records of the Ash Kan Derby don't exist, but it is known that future Indy 500 drivers Don Freeland and Troy Ruttman (then 15 years old) raced there. A fatality pretty much brought the Derby to a close.

But there were many more oval tracks in and around Los Angeles. Gilmore Stadium, Bonelli Stadium in Saugus, and occasionally the L.A. Coliseum and the Rose Bowl in Pasadena played host to the elitist professional midget races. And when midget racing was at its absolute peak in popularity, race organizers weren't about to let in a bunch of mongrel hot rods and their drivers and crewmembers wearing dirty jeans and T-shirts. What to do?

Most of those young men had returned from war duty, and for the first time in many years they had a little extra money in their pockets (remember, prior to World War II America and the rest of the world had experienced more than 10 years of economic depression). Most of all, those young men craved excitement. In 1946, building contractor Emmett Malloy and race car owner Bill Dehler proposed to Judge Frank Carrell that building

Floyd Roberts raced this rather crude Ford-powered roadster at Jefferies Ranch, shown here in about 1935. Roberts also raced at Indy five times, including a win in 1938. Many of the great pre- and postwar California drivers who competed at Indianapolis got their start at West Coast roadster races. *Nordskog Family Collection*

Racers vie for position during the start of the Ash Kan Derby, held in a vacant lot in San Bernardino, east of Los Angeles. Sadly, all that vacant land today is filled with housing tracts and strip malls. *Dave "Monk" Thormin Collection*

Bonelli Stadium in Saugus, California, was an early home of roadster racing in Southern California. The cars line up before a race for driver introductions. Among them are Jack McGrath (16), Bob Cross (105), Len Knollhoff (17), Gil Ayala (18), Andy Linden (20), Gordon Reid (36), Jay Frank (48), and Bud Van Maanen (64). *Dave "Monk" Thormin Collection*

a racetrack on his land at 174th Street and Vermont Avenue in Gardena, a suburb south of Los Angeles, would help get racers off the street. But more than just a racetrack was necessary. A sanctioning organization was needed to implement and sustain the racing. A meeting was held in engine-builder Babe Ouse's garage to form a new type of association. Chuck "Satan" Leighton was elected its president, but turned down the position because he wanted to race and didn't think it proper for a driver in competition to run the events. Instead, Johnny Walker, owner of the timing system, was elected president. Since "hot rod" was still a dirty word to the public (*Hot Rod* was still a year and a half away from its first edition), the boys made sure not to mention it in their promotions. Instead, they chose the straightforward name California Roadster Association (CRA). Charter members included Ralph Ruttman and his son, Troy, Pat Flaherty, Jack McGrath, Manuel Ayulo, the Rathmann brothers, Don Freeland, Joe and Walt James, and Jimmy Davies—all names destined to become famous nationally.

The era of true track roadster racing began when the CRA held its inaugural event at Judge Carrell's track, named Gardena Bowl (later Carrell Speedway), on Labor Day, 1946. It is said that 50 cars tried to qualify, most of which had never seen the inside of a racetrack before. Many of the boys drove their roadsters to the track, pulled off the windshields and headlights, stuck their '39 Ford transmissions in second gear, and had at it. A feature story in that first race's printed program demonstrated that hot rodding was taking off in all directions as hot rodders sought their favorite niche. If the car entry had previously run at the dry lakes, its top speed was listed. McGrath's car, No. 4, and Ayulo's No. 44 were listed at 124 miles per hour, with Connie Weidell's No. 41 tops at 128 miles per hour. Further evidence of this wild era is the fact that George Barris and Gil Ayala, both known for their customizing and bodywork talents, tried their hands at track roadster racing.

Experience paid off at Carrell's first race when Wally Pankratz, driving Rudy Ramos' channeled '29, won the first 20-lap main event. Pankratz had raced at Southern Ascot before

Jack McGrath raced this '32 Ford at Gardena Speedway in September 1946 during a CRA event. Racing in the background is Manuel Ayulo in another '32. Interestingly, both drivers shared the ride in the *Hinkle Special* to finish third at Indy in 1951. Both drivers were from California. *Taylor Family Collection*

Jack Bayliss leads Manny Ayulo and Jack McGrath in a cloud of dust at Gardena Bowl (later Carrell Speedway) in September 1946. Roadster racing proved popular during the postwar era, as evidenced by the large spectator crowd. *Taylor Family Collection*

Bert Letner was a member of the Road Runners when he ran this car in Class C Roadster in '47. It was powered by a Mercury with Elco Twin heads and ignition, Edelbrock manifold, and Weber cam. The car finished first in class in June with a 125.87-mile-per-hour speed. After that, it was all downhill at the lakes. On the CRA circuit the car finished first in points and wore No. 19 in 1948 with Troy Ruttman driving. A Joe Henning drawing of the car graces the cover of Dick Wallen's *Roaring Roadsters* book.

the war and his brother, Bob, was a star midget driver and car builder. It became evident early on that when it came to track racing the driver was every bit as important as the roadster. The story was different at the lakes where, as long as common sense prevailed, a driver could get even an ill-handling car through the timing traps. Rather than a technical exercise of who could build the fastest car within a framework of class rules, successful track roadsters required a combination of power, handling, and savvy driving. From the beginning it was pretty easy to see who the *real* race car drivers were in the field. After three or four races and the first CRA fatality at Bonelli (Saugus) in October, many of the would-be chauffeurs hung up their goggles and went back to the street and the dry lakes meets or simply hired a driver at the ovals who would share in a percentage of the winnings.

Crowd estimates in the local newspapers ranged from 10,000 to 14,000 spectators at these races. No matter the exact number, track roadster racing was a hit. Before long the roadsters were welcomed at Bonelli and were invited to the track in Bakersfield and to Balboa Stadium in San Diego. By the end of '46, Jack McGrath had won the season championship and the right to carry No. 1 on his car the following season. The band of hot rodders who were formerly mostly midnight street racers had become downright respectable. Hot rodding was coming of age.

Indeed, things were changing fast for the hot rod crowd. For 1947, the CRA added a rule that declared cars couldn't race with windshield brackets in place. The days of driving to the

This Northern California track roadster started life as a 1927 Chevrolet. It's seen beside the grandstand at the Oakland Mile in 1941. On occasion this car also ran with a 1923 Ford Model T roadster body, showing the versatility of these lightweight race cars. *Mario Baffico Collection*

track and stripping windshield and headlights to make the car suitable for racing were over. Besides, Ayulo and McGrath, who shared a garage in the Silver Lake district northwest of downtown L.A., quickly reasoned that, just as at the lakes, the smaller '27 T was much "racier" than their Deuce highboys. Placed on a lightened Model T frame (CRA rules required production frame rails) and powered by the popular 3/8x3/8 flathead V-8 engine positioned slightly rearward in the chassis for better traction, racers discovered that they had a heck of a race car.

Shortly thereafter, Jim Rathmann showed up with an in-and-out gearbox in his T, and the day of the dual-purpose hot rod was all but over. Since traction was the limiting factor and dirt-track racing tires were still a long way off, choice of engines was all over the board. There were Ford four-bangers (of both Model A and B varieties), flathead Ford sixes, Chevy and GMC six-cylinder engines, and, of course, the venerable flathead Ford V-8. The speed equipment business was quickly growing into the speed equipment industry as names like Weiand, Navarro, Edelbrock, Iskenderian, and Howard became commonplace at the roadster races as well as the lakebeds. Cylinder heads by Riley, Edmunds, and Wayne Horning catered to the inline engine builders, and Kong, Harman and Collins, and Spalding provided the ignitions.

Of course, success breeds competition, and by 1948 other racing organizations were formed. California Hot Rods, Inc. promoted events at the hallowed Gilmore Stadium. Another group, calling itself American Sports Cars, Inc., implying that roadsters were the

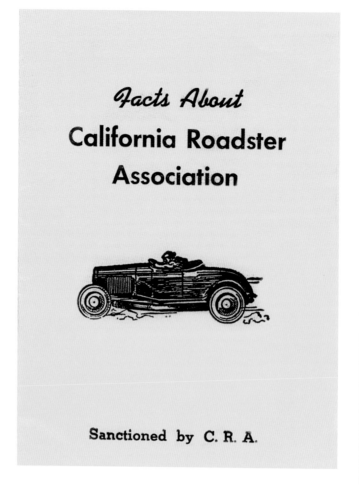

Facts About
California Roadster Association

Sanctioned by C. R. A.

(Opposite page) The Hartman/Wayne-powered GMC track roadster, shown here at Carrell Speedway in 1948, was built in just nine days. The roadster had torsion-bar suspension and a Kurtis midget nose over a Ford V8-60 radiator. Wayne Horning (far left) and John Hartman (second from right) pose with their crew. *Dan Warner Collection*

American version of the newly popular European imports, joined in, too. But the ASC's events lasted only a couple of seasons. Up north, the Northern California Roadster Racing Association had been formed in '47 and was as successful as the CRA had been in the south. Wanting a bigger piece of the action, Bay Area promoters formed Roaring Roadsters, Inc. Future Indy 500 stars Bob Sweikert, Bob Veith, and Elmer George (father of today's Indianapolis Motor Speedway president Tony George) raced with both groups.

Roadster racing flourished in other parts of the country as well. Jim Rathmann read in a racing publication about huge crowds pulled in by Andy Granatelli's Hurricane Racing Association near Chicago. Figuring that California hot rods had to be better than Midwestern hot rods, Rathmann loaded up his beautiful blue No. 16 and headed east. He did so well that Granatelli began paying him to run second once in a while, just to keep the show interesting for

Stan Dean and Earl Sadler of San Leandro, California, ran this track roadster as members of Roadster Racing, Inc., in the late 1940s. The car is seen on the trailer before an RRI race at Oakland Stadium's 5/8-mile high-banked track. The car was among those shown at the first Oakland Roadster Show in January 1950. *Mario Baffico Collection*

the spectators. Rathmann didn't want other Californians to cut in on his action so he asked his dad, who worked the CRA pit gate, to tell "the boys" that Jim was barely making it and having to work other jobs just to stay in bread and boloney. The truth was, Rathmann was making so much money racing five or six nights a week that he thought he could never spend it all. He recalls that bring-home money from that first year was more than $40,000—not bad money for a racer in 1948! The word eventually got out, however, and others, including Don Freeland and future Indy winner Pat Flaherty, "went east." Yam Oka sold his immaculate No. 8 to Granatelli and Rathmann drove it as well.

In addition to the Hurricane Racing Association, expatriated Californians ran with the Mutual Racing Association in Indiana. Mutual dated back to the '30s and their cars were a curious blend of roadster and sprint car. Dick Frazier was their local hot dog, running with a Clay Smith–built engine imported from California. Other groups, such as the Roadster Racing Associations of Oregon, Washington, Texas, and, in fact, about half the states in the Union, held roadster races, but the weather and the speed equipment industry that prevailed in California gave the CRA a huge jump on the rest of the country.

By the latter part of 1948, however, the CRA's popularity began to wane. Fatalities had received banner headlines in the Hearst-owned L.A. newspapers, and fragmented organizations vying for cars and drivers led to oversaturation; roadster, midget, big car (sprints), and stock car racing could be found seven nights a week at any of 11 tracks within a 60-mile radius of L.A. City Hall. Purses fell so much that one car owner made $95.31 as the winner's share and had to give the driver 40 percent of that! Many fans chose to simply stay home and watch wrestling on their tiny new Hoffman black-and-white television sets.

Race promoter J. C. Agajanian offered a plan. The roadsters would be forced to use roll bars and run a single carburetor and gasoline only. In addition, he paved Carrell Speedway to make it "safer." With these and other changes, Troy Ruttman repeated as season champion.

The 1949 and 1950 seasons delivered more of the same, with most of the early CRA stars running American Automobile Association (AAA) events in their bids for a chance at the Indianapolis 500. In 1950 the CRA sanctioned only 15 races.

We can't discuss track roadster racing without mention of Walt James. He and his brother, Joe, were veterans of the Ash Kan Derby. Joe was considered a better driver and had a shot at Indy before he was killed in a championship race at San Jose in 1952. Walt claims, "I talked a better race, so I had better rides." Walt was nearly killed returning from a race in Clovis, California, in October 1950. Bud Winfield, creator of the Novi and brother of Ed, the mechanical genius behind carburetors and camshafts that bore his name, lost his life in the accident, and Walt wound up in intensive care for 10 days and in traction for 2 months.

The accident proved a blessing in disguise for roadster racing, though: Walt wasn't at the CRA meeting to decline the nomination to be president, and his fellow members elected him. It proved to be a wise selection, as James used his convalescent period wisely, making telephone calls to book monthly CRA races at Carrell, Huntington Beach, and Culver City. He

The Hiatt Brothers track roadster arrives on the trailer behind the 1941 Pontiac tow car at Oakland Stadium for a race in 1948. Car owner Lonnie Hyatt of San Carlos, California, was a member of the RRI (Roadster Racing, Inc.), a Northern California roadster racing association. *Mario Baffico Collection*

All show and no go? Hardly. Bert Letner's track T is seen at the Los Angeles National Guard Armory in January 1949. The car was driven in CRA events by Troy Ruttman, who later gained fame as the 1952 Indianapolis 500 winner. *Mario Baffico Collection*

convinced track operators growing weary of follow-the-leader Kurtis-Offy midget shows and jalopy races turning into demolition derbies that the real show was the roadsters. Besides, many CRA owners were making their cars beautiful as well as fast. The Spalding brothers' No. 43 and Fred Ige's No. 100, for example, were beautiful enough to merit full features in *Hot Rod,* complete with Rex Burnett cutaways.

In fact, early in 1950 and despite declining attendance, track roadsters were popular enough that a good part of the first National Roadster Show (later to become known as the Grand National Roadster Show) in Oakland, California, was made up of track roadsters entered in the "Speedway Division." Ige's yellow roadster was awarded First Place Construction and First Place Originality, and judged third for America's Most Beautiful Roadster behind winner Bill NieKamp's street/lakes '29 Ford and Larry Neves' Oakland-based track roadster. It's amazing in today's context to realize that the first AMBR winner was nearly a race car!

Walt James' hard work began to pay off. Bob Denny won the 1951 CRA points championship in an 18-event schedule with purses averaging over $1,200. It wasn't quite like it was in the '40s, but things were looking up. The 1952 schedule was more of the same. But most of all, the CRA's prestige in the racing community grew tenfold.

Until 1956, professional auto racing on the national level was sanctioned by the American Automobile Association—or simply "Triple A"—the same folks who today help you when you break down on the highway or run out of gas. AAA ruled auto racing with an iron fist. So great was their power, including ruling over the Indianapolis 500, that drivers who raced in events not sanctioned by AAA were known as "outlaws," as if they had committed some sort of heinous crime.

In a 1952 article in the *Wall Street Journal*, AAA official Russ Catlin wrote: "We do not sanction or condone hot rod racing. It is not professional auto racing. The hot rod is a menace not only on the highway, but the speedway." Yet that year fully half of the drivers in the Indy 500—including winner Troy Ruttman, the youngest ever at age 22—had begun their careers in roadsters.

By the end of 1952, it was evident that the public's tastes were changing. They were tired of old Fords, no matter how sophisticated their engineering. The public wanted to see bona fide race cars. Seeing the handwriting on the wall, several owners gave their cars sprint car bodies and tails, allowing them to change back and forth to suit the situation. In March 1953, the CRA ran an "open competition" event at Corona, allowing sprint cars to race with the roadsters. Skee Redican won the race in veteran hot rodder (and co-founder of Ansen Automotive) Louis Senter's flathead-powered sprinter. Some people began referring to the CRA as the California *Racing* Association.

At that same time, various tracks began to shut down. Carrell Speedway was closed in 1954 and became an extension of Artesia Boulevard. Douglas Aircraft bought the Culver City Speedway site. Adding to the track roadsters' woes, the American public began its fascination with sports car road racing. On Halloween Day, 1954, 79 roadsters and sprint cars showed up

When the tires of two cars made contact with each other at speed, something bad was sure to happen. This photo is from a series taken by Eric Rickman at Oakland Speedway before he went to work with Pete Petersen. Bert Letner's Elco Twin–sponsored Model T, usually driven by Troy Ruttman, makes a safe pass down below. A lot of cool track roadsters were wasted that day. *Mario Baffico Collection*

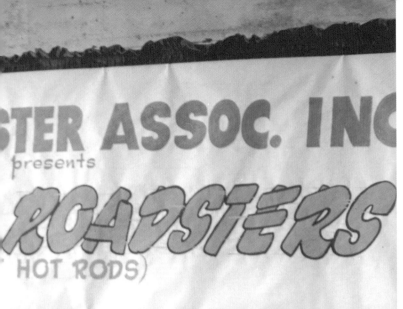

to qualify on a two-mile road circuit bladed out of an Agoura ranch north of L.A. The curious field was led by Johnny Poulsen in the former Bonneville roadster belonging to Henry and James. The smooth, oiled surface soon deteriorated to a rock garden. The cars—and drivers—were pelted by rocks, but 6,500 people sat on the hillsides to watch Jay Abney win in a sprinter powered by a Ford six-cylinder. He was followed by Scotty Cain in a Deuce highboy and eventual season champion Jack Gardner in his tube-framed track T roadster.

The 1955 and 1956 seasons saw fewer and fewer roadsters, and more and more sprint cars. In 1955 the CRA's name was officially changed to California Racing Association, and the following year roadster bodies were no longer allowed. The reformulated CRA would become one of the top sprint car clubs in the country until its home track, Ascot Park (built in 1957 just south and across the street from where Carrell Speedway had stood) closed in 1990. Walt James continued to serve as president through 1970.

No doubt, the track roadsters had a great impact on American racing during the decade from 1946 through 1956. Many of the successful Indy drivers—people like Ayulo, McGrath, Freeland, George, Len Sutton, Dick Rathmann, and Ed Elisian—began their careers in track roadsters. Even legendary car builder and chief mechanic A. J. Watson started off by crafting a '27 T track roadster. Indy 500 winners Troy Ruttman, Bob Sweikert, Pat Flaherty, Jimmy Bryan, Rodger Ward, and Jim Rathmann all came from the roadster ranks as well. By 1957, most of the roadsters had been converted to sprint cars, their bodies simply discarded. Fortunately, a few have survived and have been lovingly restored. Many of their styling cues, such as nerf bars, hand-formed noses, and louvers are still seen on street-driven hot rods, serving as a reminder of this important chapter in American auto racing and hot rod history.

The body was removed from the Menvig-Daigh track roadster to showcase the car's chassis at the 1950 *Hot Rod* Show. Safety standards were less stringent in those days, as evidenced by the flimsy circular-shaped roll bar. The show was held at the Shrine Auditorium in Los Angeles. *Robert E. Petersen Collection*

CHAPTER 4

Charles "Scotty" Scott's clean 1923 roadster powered by a supercharged Ardun-Ford flathead V-8 was a *Hot Rod* magazine feature car. Scotty began his racing career at Muroc Dry Lake in the 1930s, and his belly tank was the first open-wheel car to get a driver into the Bonneville 200 MPH Club. *Tommy Ivo Collection*

DRAG RACING

Into the future, a quarter-mile at a time

By Dain Gingerelli

IN ABOUT THE TIME IT TAKES YOU TO READ THIS SENTENCE, a Top Fuel dragster can travel from a standing start to over 330 miles per hour. In terms of elapsed time, that's about 4.5 seconds, and the distance covered equates to a quarter-mile, which also happens to be the length of a certified National Hot Rod Association (NHRA) drag strip.

Despite such mind-boggling performance, drag racing is sometimes perceived as a rather simple form of motorsport competition. You can't blame some people for feeling that way, either. After all, the racing remains confined to a rather small arena—a quarter-mile strip of asphalt that's as straight as a preacher's promise. Moreover, only two participants at a time are allowed onto the track. Clearly, drag racing continues to be a microcosm of automobile racing's big picture.

But, as the saying goes, don't judge a book by its cover. Today's Top Fuel dragsters encompass some of the most advanced technology in motorsports, with onboard diagnostics to provide precise measurements of a dragster's performance. It takes more than just a driver with a lead foot driving a car laden with horsepower to travel 330-plus miles per hour in the standing quarter-mile. It takes pinpoint technology, too, and hot rodders have spent more than half a century developing it.

To truly appreciate the origins of drag racing, it's best to have a clear understanding of today's Top Fuel dragsters, considered the pinnacle of the sport. Engine builders calculate that a typical supercharged Top Fuel V-8 engine—with pistons the size of coffee cans—produces in excess of 5,000 horsepower. The supercharger alone generates as much as 32 pounds of boost per square inch, and fuel pressure is in the neighborhood of 300 psi, necessary to feed enough nitro methane to the 32 separate fuel nozzles scattered throughout the intake system. (Generally there are eight nozzles in the injector hat, eight positioned in the intake manifold, and 16—two per cylinder—nestled within the cylinder heads.) The flame front's temperature in each cylinder can reach 7,050 degrees Fahrenheit, and ignition is generated by dual magnetos that supply 44 amps to each spark plug—the equivalent output from an arc welder.

It gets wilder. The engine has a redline of about 9,500 rpm, but because the race itself lasts only about 4.5 seconds, the engine's total crankshaft revolutions during the actual race are only about 550. Even so, the spark plugs are pretty much melted before the halfway mark, and the remaining nitro methane fuel is consumed only because the engine is dieseling from compression, not to mention the heat from exhaust valves that are glowing red at 1,400 degrees Fahrenheit. Only by shutting off the fuel flow—or a calamitous roar of broken parts—will the engine shut down.

Oddly, though, such speeds should never have happened. That is, it never should have happened, according to what the editors of *Rods and Customs* wrote in Vol. 1, No. 1 (later, with the second issue, the magazine became known as *Rod & Custom*, as it remains today). In 1953, shortly after attending a weekend drag race at Paradise Mesa—a converted airstrip near San Diego, California—the editors stated in their report: "The Sunday before we attended, one rail job was officially clocked at a little over 140 mph. The maximum speed, as calculated by formula, that any internal combustion engine . . . while driving through its wheels will ever attain in the quarter mile is 147 mph."

Obviously, those calculations were a bit wrong, as Kenny Bernstein (the first to eclipse 300 miles per hour in 1992) and scores of other racers subsequently proved.

But *R&C*'s bold prediction about absolute top speed in the quarter-mile illustrates today how naive the early drag racing pioneers were when it came to understanding a form of competition that was still very much in its infancy. Indeed, 50 years ago there was much to learn about drag racing, which had yet to be recognized as an amateur sport, let alone a form of professional competition.

Even today, when compared to most other motorsports, professional drag racing is deemed young. According to most authorities, the first organized meet was held in 1949, but

it wasn't until the mid-1950s that the sport achieved true professional status when the NHRA sanctioned its first Nationals in Kansas. Even then there was little money to be made, so most "professional" drivers maintained their full-time jobs during the weekdays.

Yet the art of drag racing, in which two cars square off to see which is quicker from a standing start, can trace its roots to the time of crank-start engines and wood-spoke wheels. If you've read one undocumented account, you've probably read a dozen similar stories by automotive journalists who have waxed nostalgic about two "nameless" drivers who—those journalists could only assume—met on the street in their runabout roadsters. After exchanging glances, so most accounts will tell you, both drivers screeched (as only a Ford Model T or some other natty early-age automobile could do) down the street, disappearing into a cloud of oily smoke and dust to determine which of them had the faster car. From that showdown was borne the street racer-cum-drag racer.

But the documented story about *organized* drag racing originates in the 1930s when young men gathered with their hot rods at Muroc Dry Lake (now officially known as Rogers Dry Lake, located in the heart of Edwards Air Force Base) in California's vast Mojave Desert. It was there that rodders lined up, sometimes eight abreast, to sprint down the flat, hard-packed, dry alkaline lakebed. The racing went in the following manner: A pilot car paced the racers at about 30 miles per hour until they crossed the start line. At that point the race began, usually lasting about a mile to a predetermined finish line.

As you can imagine, the losers of that sprint across the dry lakebed were left steering blindly in a cloud of fine alkaline powder. Obviously, this posed a hazard for the trailing drivers who were literally encapsulated by the ensuing dust storm, so the racers sought technology to solve the problem. The solution rested with an electronic timing apparatus that used a series of lights to measure the time it took for a car to pass through the beam of one light to the next. Using this technology, the cars could race individually, so that nobody had to drive in another's rooster-tail dust cloud. At the end of the day, after all of the cars had made at least one pass, the car with the fastest time (or speed) was deemed the winner. But the dry lakes

Sam Matsuda and his 1947 Chevrolet Aero-Sedan are seen in this retouched publicity shot touting speed parts for Harry Warner's Wayne Manufacturing Company. The door-slammer had a Wayne 12-port head with 9:1 compression, three carbs, and a Wayne C-304 cam. It turned 102 miles per hour at the Santa Ana Drags and ran 118 miles per hour at El Mirage Dry Lake during a Russetta meet. *Dan Warner Collection*

racing measured top speed only. The thrill of side-by-side competition was missing. Also, hot rodders in other parts of the country didn't have the long stretches of open country afforded to Southern Californians with their dry lakes, so they couldn't even race for top-speed honors. For that matter, not every Southern California hot rodder had the resources, or the ambition, to venture more than 100 miles northeast to the Mojave Desert just to see if his car was faster, or quicker, than the next guy's. So street racing among the hot rod crowd continued to thrive. Especially in Southern California.

Perhaps the biggest step toward establishing organized drag racing occurred a few years after World War II—1949, to be precise. That's when a hot rod club known as the Santa Barbara Acceleration Association sanctioned an organized drag meet at Goleta Airport. The racing was held on an abandoned two-lane service road. That historic event also included what could be construed as the first "grudge" match. The showdown pitted two well-known dry lakes racers, Fran Hernandez and Tom Cobbs, against each other.

Mickey Thompson tries out what many consider to be the first slingshot dragster with a narrowed rear axle at the strip in Pomona, California. Thompson's car first ran in 1954. Obviously, he was onto something special. *Robert E. Petersen Collection*

Cobbs' Ford roadster was powered by a supercharged flathead V-8, while Hernandez was experimenting with nitro methane fuel in his '32 Ford, also powered by a "flattie" V-8. In the end, the fuel-fed car prevailed, becoming what could be unofficially deemed drag racing's first Top Fuel Eliminator.

Shortly after Goleta, a handful of rodders in the Memphis, Tennessee, area staged their own drag race. The Memphis Rodders Car Club has the distinction of promoting the first drag race east of the Mississippi River, and in the process you might say that drag racing had become a national sport.

Thanks to Goleta and Memphis, the seeds had been planted, but it wasn't until the following year that a sprout popped up, this time in Orange County, California. As the name suggests, Orange County was a region awash with orange trees that entrenched the community in Southern California's vast citrus industry. In addition to the hundreds of orange groves, the flat, wide-open spaces in Orange County 50 years ago were consumed with farm fields that supported various other crops as well, including beans, strawberries, and lettuce. The flat farmland lent itself well to the World War II war effort in another way, too. That's when the U.S. military built several airfields in Orange County to train fighter pilots. Among the airstrips built were Mile Square Airfield (in present-day Fountain Valley) and Santa Ana Airfield, later to become Orange County Airport. Today,

The *Nesbett's Orange Special* leaves the line at a strip in Southern California. Nesbett's was the soft drink company that sponsored the dragster, making this drag race team one of the first to have a non-automotive sponsor. *Tony Nancy Collection*

There were no bad seats at Lions Drag Strip, often referred to by locals as The Beach. The drag strip, owned by the local Lions Club and first operated by Mickey Thompson, was located in Long Beach, California, where the fresh, thick ocean air made for good horsepower. *Tommy Ivo Collection*

Orange County Airport is known as John Wayne Airport, and Mile Square Airfield is a municipal park.

As the war clouds subsided and peace reigned upon the land, the military's need for Orange County's airfields diminished. Almost immediately after the war, Mile Square was relegated to emergency landing strip status only and the wide asphalt runways were called upon only by U.S. military—and civilian, if necessary—aircraft in need of emergency landing. Once the local hot rodders caught wind of the situation, they concocted ways to sneak onto the abandoned air base to conduct their moonlight drags on the smooth asphalt runways.

Al Voegtly, a member of the Clutchers Car Club (established in Santa Ana, California), recalled, "Oh, we'd sneak on there (Mile Square) and run until the MPs [military police] would show up and chase us off." Voegtly said that on a good night the hot rodders could sneak in about a dozen or so passes, usually running several cars abreast, à la early Muroc.

Eventually a few of the more responsible hot rodders, led by Wally Parks, who would later gain recognition as editor of *Hot Rod* magazine and as the NHRA's first president, attempted

Before he helped form Dragmaster, Jim "Jazzy" Nelson built and raced *The Outlaw*, seen here at Bakersfield, California. This dragster, powered by a pair of Mercury flathead V-8s, was an interesting combination in 1957. *Tony Nancy Collection*

to sanction an organized event at Mile Square Airfield. But before the racers had a chance to show how responsible they were, the local police shut them down. So it was back to the streets, or the dry lakes, or nothing.

The local race crowd during that time included two young men, Creighton Hunter and C. J. "Pappy" Hart. Hunter was an oil salesman (he helped introduce Castrol to the U.S. market prior to World War II, and specialized in promoting Kendall after the war) who had made several contacts within the motorsport community. Hart owned and operated an automotive service station at the corner of First Street and Harbor Boulevard in the nearby city of Santa Ana. Both men were avid hot rodders.

One day, while making a sales call at Hart's garage, the topic of the aborted Mile Square event entered their discussions. Years later Hunter recalled, "C. J. and I were talking about forming a drag race. We didn't have insurance, but I said, 'I know Frank does.' So we (Creighton, C. J., and Frank) became partners."

"Frank" happened to be a local motorcycle race promoter and shop owner named Frank Stillwell. Hunter knew that Stillwell had promoted several successful motorcycle dirt-track

Tommy Ivo's Buick-powered rail lifts the front end while launching off the line against the Dragmaster rail in 1959. The Dragmaster car was powered by a small-block Chevrolet bored and stroked to 328 cubic inches and had a front-mount GMC blower. Dragmaster specialized in building dragster frames and was owned by Jim Nelson and Dode Martin. *Tommy Ivo Collection*

races at a nearby horse track, which also meant that he had access to race promoter liability insurance, a necessity even during those halcyon days.

Hunter and Hart met with Stillwell, and the three young men decided to promote a drag race. As fortune had it, they had a friend and ally at nearby Orange County Airport, a facility that the military had recently turned over for civilian use. That friend was Eddie Martin, who, with his brothers, John and Floyd, operated Martin Aviation. The Martins' hangar was situated on the west side of the facility, adjacent to the west runway that was used primarily by private companies and pilots. The east runway was reserved for daily public and commercial use, and had become the predominant strip for takeoffs and landings.

The Martins were among the early aviators in Orange County, and by 1950 had built a favorable reputation among the community's civic and business leaders. Eddie Martin suggested that the wannabe drag race promoters present their idea to his friend and mayor, the

honorable Cortney Chandler. After discussion, it was agreed that Hunter, Hart, and Stillwell could use the west runway for their event. The scheduled date was July 2, 1950.

With little time to prepare, there was no pre-race advertising campaign to speak of. That they had little money played a factor, too. Their solution was to print small posters that they nailed to telephone poles in the nearby communities. Immediately, they were called on the carpet by the local authorities. As Hunter explains today, "The city got on us for contaminating the city." So they dutifully removed the posters, but by that time word had spread about the forthcoming event, which became known as the Santa Ana Drags.

No records were kept regarding attendance and entry figures of that first event, but the three entrepreneurs made enough money that Sunday afternoon to cover expenses. Spectators paid 50 cents to stand along the track and watch the racing, while the entry fee for racing was set at a buck; racers were allowed as many passes down the quarter-mile as they could manage before the track closed at night. Tech inspection? Says Hunter, who was assigned the task that first day, "I'd look to see that they had four (good) tires. It was not real technical, but it got serious later on. All the cars were safe back then, if you know what I mean." In short, attorneys had yet to discover the bonanza that potential racing hazards offered.

As for the racers, they felt that they had struck it rich. The airport runway offered smooth asphalt to race on, there was an orderly process to queue up for side-by-side runs against a chosen adversary, a single flag starter controlled the racing, and, best of all, nobody had to worry

Jocko Johnson's streamline dragster turned the drag race community on its ear in 1959. So radical was this Chrysler-powered car that *Sports Cars Illustrated* was the only national publication to do a story on it that year. *Tommy Ivo Collection*

Aviator Chuck Yeager once said that aviation progress is marked by big black holes in the ground. The same can almost be said about drag racing. Here, in 1960, Tommy Ivo took the plunge when his dragster had trouble stopping after a run at the drag strip in Concord, Delaware. *Tommy Ivo Collection*

about getting busted by the police or MPs. Norman Rockwell couldn't have painted a better picture for the drag-thirsty hot rodders.

There was no timing apparatus, nor were there qualifying or elimination brackets, either. No prize money or trophies, for that matter. Simply, you ran as fast and hard as you could to be the first to the finish line in your match race. Your reward was beating the other car and, with it, brag-

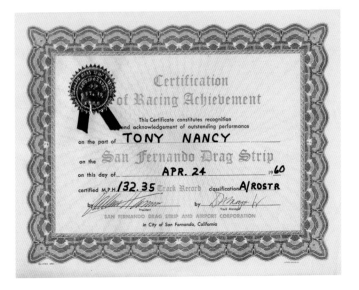

ging rights back in the pits and, later, on the street. Incidentally, on opening day the finish line was positioned nearly a third of a mile from the start line. The quarter-mile distance would be established at a later meet, but for now the Santa Ana Drags was run-whatcha-brung fun.

The inaugural Santa Ana Drags was an overwhelming success, and the city even made money by netting a percentage of the gate. The city's administrators gave Hunter, Hart, and Stillwell the green light to promote on a weekly basis and overnight drag racing had an organized event that sanctioned meets on a regular schedule. They even hired a track announcer, Don Tuttle, who later gained stature as the resident motorsports authority for the *Santa Ana Register* newspaper (now the *Orange County Register*).

The trifecta partnership experimented with the starting procedure, too. The original format was to use standing starts, controlled by a flagman who dropped a green flag to begin each race. This was acceptable, except for one minor glitch: the clutches and spindly rear ends in the cars couldn't withstand the abuse of sudden acceleration. Clutches burned and gears sheared, so the promoters tried rolling starts. Remember, though, the airport was flat and, in fact, located in the flood plain of the nearby Santa Ana River (which predictably dried up every summer). Fortunately, the U.S. Air Force had used the north end of the runway for bombing practice. According to Hunter, a circle was painted at the end of the airstrip, where the fighter bombers dropped their phony bombs (casings packed with white powder, presumably flour) to practice their accuracy. A clean target was necessary to judge subsequent bombing runs, so the ground crew had built up the portion of the runway where the circle target was located, allowing the powdered flour to be easily swept away by ground-grunts.

The raised target site—no more than a foot high at its peak—gave Hart, Hunter, and Stillwell an idea. Why not position the racers on the dome, let them roll forward, coasting toward the starting line? Then, as they simultaneously approached the starter about 50 feet later, wave them off to officially start the race. At that point the drivers could pop the clutches and go! This process, so everybody believed, would be easy on the equipment and fair to the racers.

Ten years after drag racing's first continuous program opened at Santa Ana Airport, it was still common to find racing at airports across the country. This certificate, awarded to Tony Nancy for setting a class record, was presented by the San Fernando Drag Strip and Airport Corporation. *Tony Nancy Collection*

Tony Nancy works on what was to become *The Wedge*, one of the first successful rear-engine dragsters. Nancy was an innovator, willing to try new ideas, and his working conditions were a far cry from the sterile lab-like facilities race teams enjoy today. *Tony Nancy Collection*

Hart, et al, forgot one thing about racers: they love to take advantage of the unfair advantage. As you might guess, the rolling starts turned into roaring starts, and many were the racer who jumped the gun. After an abominable attempt, they scratched the idea and resumed standing starts, in the process letting evolution continue its course. If the sport was to survive, the racers would have to develop better equipment, that's all there was to it. (Which, as it turned out, they did, creating a whole new high-performance industry. But that's another story.)

By the third event the promoters employed J. Otto Crocker's renowned and respected timing lights. Crocker, a member of the San Diego Roadster Club, had developed a workable and accurate timing system a few years earlier that measured top speed for racing on the dry lakes. His lights readily adapted to the drags, and Santa Ana competitors now knew just how

Eddie Hill ran this double-double dragster in 1961. It had two supercharged Pontiac engines that put the power to the pavement through two pairs of slicks. *Tommy Ivo Collection*

fast—or slow—their cars were in the standing *three-tenths* mile. It wasn't until several meets later that the promoters settled on the quarter-mile distance. (It's worth noting that Crocker's lights were incapable of measuring elapsed time for the complete run. Again, that technology would come later.)

Among the fastest at the third meet was local boy Al Keys, who posted a 103.42-mile-per-hour run. The only problem, as far as the hot rod crowd was concerned, was that Keys rode a *motorcycle*. Keys piloted Chet Herbert's Harley-Davidson, a bike with an 81-cubic-inch engine built by tuning wizard Ron Felkner. The bike also was sponsored by none other than Frank Stillwell. Herbert, who later claimed fame for building and selling performance automotive camshafts, affectionately called his Harley *The Beast*. The motorcycle's moniker was well earned, too, because *The Beast* was clocked at 158 miles per hour on nearby El Mirage Dry Lake, thus earning the unofficial title as the "fastest bike on earth."

The Beast, with Keys in the saddle, proved to be the machine to beat every week at Santa Ana. Ironically, it was *The Beast's* incredible speed (at the time) that led to the evolution of the rail dragster as we know it today.

As the story goes, hot rodder Dick Kraft was among those racers determined to dethrone *The Beast* at Santa Ana. To do so, he had to find a way to squeeze more top speed from his modified roadster. Kraft, nicknamed Krafty Dick by his peers, realized that weight played a factor in how *quickly* a car—or bike—launched off the starting line. The solution, reasoned

Krafty Dick, was to eliminate weight from his car, so off came the roadster's Model T body. On July 30, 1950, Dick Kraft showed up at the Santa Ana Drags with four wheels attached to a cobbled-up frame and a hopped-up Ford flathead V-8 engine for power. A single seat held Krafty Dick in place, plus his car retained the normal array of foot pedals and steering column, not to mention its cowl section and small fuel tank. And that was about it. Thus was born the first rail dragster. Despite the noble effort, Kraft lost to Keys.

C. J. Hart had a tough time living with the idea of a driver being exposed like that (as if the tin body would save him in a crash!), so he instructed Kraft to install a roll bar for protection. Once again Krafty Dick lived up to his nickname, looping above him a roll bar made of lightweight electrical conduit. After all, less weight translated to more horsepower. Once again, he set out to slay *The Beast*.

Eventually *The Bug*, as Krafty's car was called, bit *The Beast*, and Kraft made it to the final round against Tom Cobbs' stripped coupe. The Bug won that race too, and was clocked at 109 miles per hour, thus earning the distinction of being the first rail dragster to win Top Eliminator honors.

In reality, Herbert's *Beast* had served as the rabbit that helped the car crowd chase the top speed figure beyond 120 miles per hour in the quarter-mile. Among the early Santa Ana Drags runners who helped notch quarter-mile speeds above 120 miles per hour during those

Two Fiat Topolinos blast off the starting line at the NHRA Indy Nationals in 1961. These short-wheelbase cars packed a big punch, so they always put on a great show. *Tommy Ivo Collection*

wild times were Don Nicholson, who 13 years later became known as Dyno Don, and Calvin Rice, a man destined to be the NHRA's first Top Fuel national champion in 1955.

The Santa Ana Drags were only the beginning, and within a year additional tracks opened in other parts of the country. Among them were drag strips in Hayward, California (promoted by the Rod Benders and Benderettes), Akron, Ohio (by that city's legendary Cam Jammers), and in Caddo Mills, Texas (by the Chapparals). Caddo Mills also was the site where the first elapsed time (E.T.) was recorded for a standing-start run—John Lovelean became the sport's first Top Eliminator with an official E.T., posting a time of 13.15 seconds through the quarter-mile.

By the end of 1951 Southern California racers had another drag strip, this one in the San Fernando Valley just northeast of Los Angeles. It was followed by strips in Fontana and Saugus.

The Saugus facility, located on the Six-S Air Park runway, proved unique. The racing, promoted by Lou Baney and Louie Senter, was confined to the airport's short 2,600-foot-long runway. This abbreviated distance compromised the shutdown area, so the promoters organized a flag crew at the end of the strip, which happened to terminate into an adjoining highway. When a racer made a pass, the flag crew stopped traffic on the highway so that, in the event a race car couldn't stop within the given distance, he wouldn't pose a hazard on the highway (say, where *are* those attorneys, anyway?).

By the early 1960s, smoking tires and wheel stands by rail dragsters were rather common sights at drag strips across the country. This one took place at San Fernando Drag Strip in 1963. *Tony Nancy Collection*

Baney and Senter were also among the first promoters to promote their product in the spirit of Barnum & Bailey. Realizing that Santa Ana had many of Southern California's fastest racers, Baney and Senter advertised cash awards for a forthcoming race to lure some of the speed giants to Saugus. When Santa Ana racer Art Chrisman got wind of the $175 purse, he loaded his dragster and headed to Saugus, where he claimed Top Eliminator award, plus a bundle of cash (remember, this was 1951).

Another pioneer event with an interesting story was the short-lived drag strip promoted by the Denver Timing Association (DTA). The DTA had negotiated with the Colorado Highway Patrol to use a section of a new and yet-to-be-opened stretch of highway for their race. The date was July 29, 1951, and it marked the first time that the timing lights were located equal-distance before and after the finish line, giving a true measure of the car's top speed at the end of the quarter-mile.

Tommy Ivo always managed to draw a crowd, especially when he had mechanical problems, as he did here at San Fernando Drag Strip. His engine is minus the oil pan, and he's working on the transmission. Note the detail in this Kent Fuller dragster chassis. *Tommy Ivo Collection*

Former *Hot Rod* editor Ray Brock interviews Don Prudhomme and Keith Black, two members of the famous Greer-Black-Prudhomme Top Fuel team. Prudhomme did the driving and Black built the engines. *Robert E. Petersen Collection*

A blown clutch could spell disaster for a Top Fuel dragster. Famous hot rod and race photographer Steve Reyes caught this action, which also shows how much rear slicks grow from centrifugal force. *Tony Nancy Collection*

Perhaps one of the more momentous events in drag racing history occurred on April 13, 1953, when the newly formed NHRA sanctioned its first drag race. The event was held on the Pomona Drag Strip, the same racetrack that the NHRA uses today for its famous Winternationals championship events.

The NHRA's first event attracted more than 16,000 spectators who came to see 375 cars complete 850 passes down the quarter-mile. Finally, drag racing had a sanctioning body that offered a uniform set of rules and regulations. The sport was on its way, and the following year the NHRA sanctioned 166 events at tracks across the country.

Buoyed by the NHRA, the sport grew at a fantastic rate, and by 1955 the first Nationals were held at Great Bend, Kansas. During that four-day meet (September 29 to October 2), drag racing reached a new level of professionalism. Chrisman went 145.16 miles per hour in a single-engine car, while the meet's top speed was snatched by Lloyd Scott in the *Howard & Weiand Special* dual-engine dragster, posting a terminal speed of 151.00 miles per hour—the field had eclipsed the ceiling posed by *Rods and Customs*, and even managed to surpass the halfway mark on the road to Bernstein's record run of 1992. Scott was also quickest through the traps at the first NHRA Nats, stopping the clocks in 10.48 seconds.

However, rain cancelled the meet before the finals could be run. The NHRA elected to stage the Top Fuel Finals the following month in sunny Phoenix, Arizona. There, in the crisp desert air, Calvin Rice won Top Eliminator honors with a speed and E.T. of 143.95 miles per hour and 10.30 seconds.

That same year Lions Drag Strip opened in Long Beach, California, and its weekly program was administered by a young racer named Mickey Thompson. With two permanent drag strips in the Los Angeles area, racers could go to Lions on Saturday, then head to Santa Ana the next day. And with the NHRA setting up headquarters in Los Angeles and sanctioning the annual Winternationals in nearby Pomona, Southern California became the hub for drag racing in America.

National attendance at NHRA events in 1955 surpassed 570,000, and there were nearly 40,000 entries at races throughout the country. By 1960 there were 83 NHRA-approved drag strips that accounted for more than 900 races and attracted over a million spectators. Within the next five years more than three million spectators passed through turnstiles at 136 tracks that promoted 1,913 NHRA-sanctioned events.

And while attendance figures rose, the E.T.s on the drag strip continually dropped. By 1960 Leonard Harris, Top Eliminator at the Detroit Nationals, posted an E.T. of 9.65 seconds. His speed was 165.13 miles per hour. The following year Pete Robinson banged out an 8.92/169.49 combo, and within four years Don Prudhomme kicked top speed at the NHRA Nationals—by then held annually at Indianapolis Raceway Park—to 207.33 miles per hour.

Nobody even contemplated going 300 miles per hour when Prudhomme posted his 207 speed, but the point was clear: drag racing was here to stay. Since those early days, drag racing has blossomed into a professional form of motorsport equal to any other national championship series in America. Nobody's yet talking about going 400 miles per hour, but based on drag racing's storied past, ya gotta wonder.

CHAPTER 5

SPREADING
THE WORD

Magazines and car shows create
a catalyst to go national

By Ken Gross

PRIOR TO WORLD WAR II, hot rodding wasn't limited only to supervised amateur competition. Much to the distress of tabloid newspapers, the local police, and countless concerned parents, a large number of young men modified their old cars and irresponsibly raced them on the streets. The resulting mayhem, along with frequent headline-grabbing injuries and violent deaths, soon made the term "hot rod" a pejorative. That perception would change, but not for years.

Although most people think *Hot Rod* magazine was the first to chronicle the sport, *HRM* had a short-lived predecessor in the halcyon years before World War II erupted. *Throttle* magazine opened up in Los Angeles in January 1941. Available for just 10 cents, its 12-page, full-size first issue was printed in black and white, with a red cover band over an Art Deco *Throttle* logo. Also, prewar publications such as *Automobile Racing* included accounts from racing on the dry lakes, but these stories were of lesser importance than the magazine's main subject matter: closed-circuit racing.

They didn't call him "TV Tommy" Ivo for nothing. Here, the television celebrity-cum-rodder is filmed with his T-bucket roadster. This photo session was included in an issue of *Car Craft* magazine. *Tommy Ivo Collection*

THE RILEY 4 PORT RACING HEAD

The new **Riley** 4 port racing head is the culmination of sixteen years development of the dual intake valve rocker arm cylinder head for racing engines, built around the four cylinder B Ford block.

The new **head casting** is heat treated aluminum which provides not only less weight than cast iron heads but assures improved heat control.

The **two intake valves** per cylinder are seated upon bronze valve seats.

The Riley 4 Port Racing Head and Carburetors

Steel inserts for 18 M.M. spark plugs are spline locked into the aluminum to prevent turning and stripped threads.

Provision is made for a header type water outlet manifold on top of the cylinder head.

Four 1¾" diameter round intake ports are provided. A log type 4 port intake manifold with two Riley 2" racing carburetors provides the finest carburetion yet built for racing engines.

Compression ratio is 10 to 1 minimum and 12 to 1 maximum.

PERFORMANCE OF THE RILEY RACING HEAD

Motors equipped with **Riley** 4 port Racing Heads and carburetors have consistently proven their ability to win against equipment costing many times the price we ask for our equipment. We have without question the fastest rocker arm head yet made for a Ford motor and our prices are the lowest for a really first class racing head combination.

Now a word about Riley's improved combustion chamber. This combustion chamber design combined with the dual intake valve arrangement gives extremely high turbulence, and with the central spark

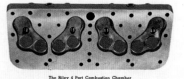

plug arrangement, results in extremely fast firing. It is only necessary to carry a spark advance of thirty to thirty-five degrees at full motor revolutions. 18 M.M. spark plugs are used.

Complete motor building instructions, together with blueprints, are furnished with each of our cylinder heads.

The Riley 4 Port Combustion Chamber

(Above left) The granddaddy of all rod magazines was *Throttle*. Unfortunately, it lived a short life, perhaps due to America's entry into World War II. *Throttle* was born, and it died, in 1941. *Jim Miller Collection*

(Above right) In 1947, George Riley was still producing parts for the old Ford four-bangers. This page is from his 1947 catalog. A complete four-port head with intake manifold, carburetors, head gasket, and cam cost $450 for a Model A or B Ford. *Don Ferrara Collection*

Throttle focused on amateur circle track and dry lakes racing. Advertisers like Tommy Thickstun, Vic Edelbrock Sr., Eddie Meyer, and Ed Winfield, to name a few, offered speed equipment for Ford fours and flathead V-8s. A popular feature, "Short Shiftings," was written in the now-quaint vernacular of the prewar era: "We've heard that a bunch of the boys from San Diego would certainly like to drag with some of the hot Los Angeles jobs, just to see how they would stack up. Wait until the first lakes meet, please fellows."

Sadly, *Throttle*'s final issue, by then 20 pages and costing 25 cents, hit the streets in December 1941, just in time for Pearl Harbor. The resulting war and subsequent paper shortages did it in. Original copies of *Throttle* are rare and hard to find today.

During the war, Veda Orr, the first—and for a while, the only—woman member of the Southern California Timing Association (SCTA), edited the *SCTA News* and mailed it to club members serving around the world. That simple club publication served to keep the hot rod spirit alive, spread the gospel to new enthusiasts, and indirectly inspire the postwar magazines that followed.

When it's questioned whether hot rod magazines or hot rod and custom car shows had the most influence on the rapid expansion of the sport, it's important to remember that both institutions played key roles. As hot rod author Dain Gingerelli observed, "When Robert E. Petersen first published *Hot Rod* magazine in January 1948, he created a communications link that brought hot rodders together from across the nation. Along with other magazines that soon followed, *HRM* provided a common dialogue, allowing like-minded young men (and a

The interior of this car that Frank Kurtis made from a wrecked 1941 Buick Century illustrates how customizers utilized parts that were available to them. Kurtis drove the car to Indy in 1948, but crashed it on the way home. After repairing it, he sold the custom car to Earl Muntz, who used it as the prototype for Kurtis' first sports car. The car was featured in the October 1948 issue of *Mechanix Illustrated*. *Mario Baffico Collection*

few women) from over the country to share ideas, and see what their counterparts were doing to *their* cars. The magazines publicized the car shows, and the impact both had on the general media was staggering. Perhaps the most notable outcome was the Muscle Car Era of the '60s and early '70s."

But we're getting ahead of our story. Let's go back to 1948 when Robert E. "Pete" Petersen, who modestly described himself as a "kid from Barstow," founded one of America's most successful magazine publishing companies. *Hot Rod* was Petersen Publishing's first national magazine, and it covered the fledgling hot rod community. It was soon followed by other related and unrelated titles, among them *Motor Trend*, *Rod & Custom*, *Car Craft*, *Guns & Ammo*, *Teen*, *Savvy*, and *Skindiving*. In the years to come, Petersen Publishing would command a dramatic effect on the growth of hot rodding in America and around the world.

HRM's timing was perfect, too. Its launch coincided with a major indoor hot rod show. "I started the First Annual Los Angeles Hot Rod Show," Bob Petersen recalled. (This was actually called the SCTA First Annual Automotive Equipment Display and Hot Rod Exposition, held January 23–25, 1948, at the L.A. Armory.) "I was with Hollywood Publicity Associates. [Earl] 'Mad Man' Muntz was one of our clients. He said, 'I want to do a big promotion. Can you do some sort of racing thing? I said, 'All the guys want a drag strip; why don't we do a hot rod show and build a drag strip with the money?' So that's how it started." The first hot rod show began as a fundraising venture, though the drag strip was never built.

Les Callahan's 1922 Dodge, built by the Barris Brothers and featuring the nose section from a Kurtis sprint car, was among the entries in the first National Roadster Show, also known as the Oakland Roadster Show. It wasn't until 1962 that the moniker "Grand" was attached to the show's title. *Mario Baffico Collection*

At the time Petersen owned a Model A that he'd purchased in 1941. "I put a '34 Ford V-8 in it. After I was in the service, I started going up to the lakes. They were actually running up there before the war; then when it ended, they started going back again. SCTA and Russetta would be running [at the lakes] and they hated each other. Wally Parks [from the SCTA] was running open cars and Lou Baney [Russetta] was running coupes; they both had a big feud going on.

"As a PR guy," continued Petersen, "I spent a lot of time going to PTA meetings and meetings with the National Safety Council . . . which was all the big deal then, so I got to know a lot of people . . . the police, too. At that time, they were going to ban hot rods. And the [hot rod] guys were doing some pretty wild things. We used to blank off Sepulveda and race down the boulevard. So they did have a problem."

Added Petersen, "Hollywood Publicity Associates was composed of people from the [movie] studios who lost their jobs after the GIs came back." Petersen's business partner and *HRM's* co-founder, Bob Lindsay, worked in film developing. "Lindsay's father had a small magazine called *Tailwaggers* for people and celebrities who owned dogs and cats. And that [association] helped us a lot.

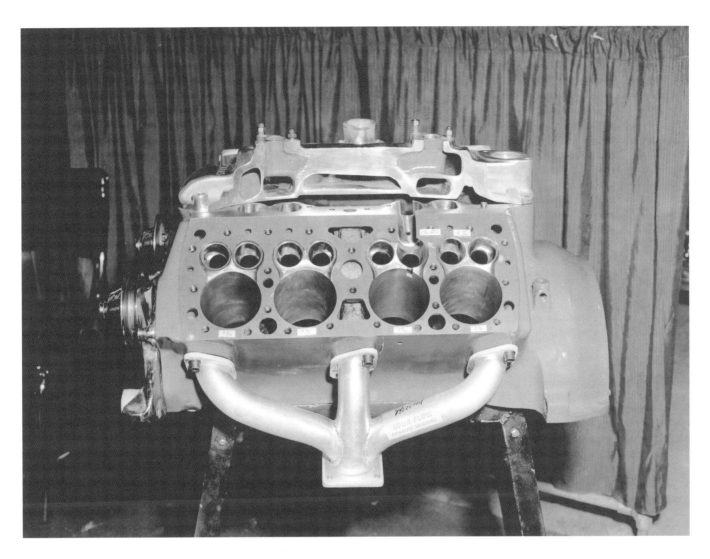

"Bob Lindsay was the business manager," explained Petersen, "and I became the sales guy and photographer. I would write stuff, too. For example, I'd interview [George] Riley and do an article on him. I went out [during late 1947] and sold booth spaces for the Hot Rod Show. We were trying to get the money to put the show on. We just had a small program with ads. But as I talked to everybody, I saw this enthusiasm to do something [more], but there wasn't anything [like a hot rod magazine]. That's what turned me on, just selling advertising to the people in the show."

It's the stuff of legends that Petersen was banned from selling *HRM* inside the Armory, so, instead, he had to sell his magazine *outside* the show. The organizers were annoyed because he had come up with a good idea and was selling magazine ads, and they didn't have a piece of that action.

As Pete later put it: "Kong Jackson asked me, 'What're these guys doing?' And I said, 'They're giving me some crap about selling my magazines.' So he said, 'I'll sell 'em.' And he did. Kong sold *Hot Rod* out front *and* in the show."

Racer Brown used this Ford V-8 flathead block in his booth at the Motorama in 1950 to help illustrate his work. Look closely and you'll see that each cylinder is bored to a different size. The collector header pipe is a Belond. *Robert E. Petersen Collection*

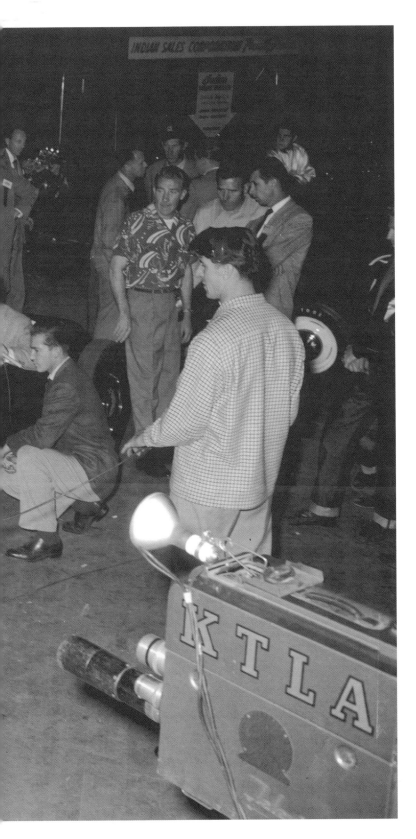

Show promoter and *Hot Rod* magazine publisher Robert E. Petersen kneels beside Kenny Grau and his roadster at the 1950 Motorama. The television camera was filming for the local Los Angeles program *City at Night*, broadcast by Channel 5 KTLA. *Robert E. Petersen Collection*

It turned out that Petersen's timing was perfect. He was ready with the first issue just as the first show got under way. There's even a show announcement on the back cover of Volume 1, Number 1. The response was terrific. "They just went crazy for it," Petersen recalled. "At first, I'd go up to the dry lakes and I'd just go from guy to guy and I'd just sell 'em, for a quarter apiece. I'd say, 'Hey, get your *Hot Rod* magazine.' I used to go to the circle tracks like Ascot, at night. Gilmore Stadium was the big deal then: 'Hot Rods at Gilmore.' I'd go down and shoot pictures during the race. During breaks I'd sell magazines. We'd pay the stadiums a nickel a copy and we'd keep 20 cents."

An announcement in the first issue noted they'd be publishing monthly. Petersen remembered: "It wasn't ever to be a one-shot. And we also started selling subscriptions [$3 annually]; we had a subscription blank, so whenever there was any place with hot rodders, I'd walk up, sell 'em a copy, and collect $3. Then we'd go around the other side and eat dinner. That's how we got our money. When we were hungry, we'd say, 'Let's go and sell some subs so we can eat.'"

HRM's early editors were not necessarily professional journalists, either. "Right from the beginning, we picked up all kinds of people," Petersen explained. "We'd say to friends, 'Hey, Joe, would you like to cover Ascot and sell magazines there?' and 'Bill, would you like to go up to San Francisco?' So we started picking up reporters and photographers. [Eric] Rickman was working for us, and a fellow named Lee Blaisdell was in early issues, doing a lot of photography."

The magazine's credibility was enhanced by articles from authentic racers like Barney Navarro and, later, Don Francisco. "Mostly we'd ghost-write for the guys," said Petersen. "I'd go talk to them and Bob did some of the writing, too. It was important to have their names. They were the heroes."

"We hired a lot of guys who were enthusiasts. We didn't have anybody who was a true writer. We just hired guys who loved the sport and I think that's what really brought it forth.

The king of the customizers, George Barris, was already a showman when this shot was taken at the Shrine Auditorium during the Motorama in 1950. The car started life as a 1949 Buick Riviera. *Robert E. Petersen Collection*

We had fellows writing the stuff who really *knew* about it. That's what the readers wanted. Not like *Esquire* where you need a guy who's an excellent writer. Our audience wanted a guy to say, 'Here's how to fix your car; here's how to do a cam; this is what overlap means; this is how to change a jet,' et cetera. They wanted to know all of this."

Indeed, Bob Petersen had a knack for selecting the right people, including his first *real* editor-in-chief. "Wally Parks is a legend. I hired him to work on *Hot Rod* before he headed up the NHRA. Ray Brock [*HRM*'s second editor] was building engines; he was a very smart guy and so was Dick Day. I just hired a lot of smart guys," Petersen said modestly. "They were all driven because they enjoyed it. We just had a great time.

"In order to build excitement in the magazine," Petersen remembered, "we built a project car. The story would run for several issues. We'd do the transmission, the bodywork, we'd paint it . . . and each chapter was in the magazine. We also came out with books on how to paint your car, how to build an engine . . . we did millions of books on that stuff. The strength of the company has always been its people—and it's still there."

The magazines worked well because they showed real people doing innovative work. "George Barris was a body man and a great creative guy," said Petersen. "He turned custom work into a big business. He and his brother, Sam, had a little two-car garage over in a bad part of town. George was at my first hot rod show. Everybody called the cars 'lead sleds.' That used to make George mad. But he dreamed up all these cars. We did a lot of magazine stories on him. He made us by doing creative things we could write about, and we made him by doing the stories. That's what happened. We all made each other. Without someone making hot manifolds, we wouldn't have a story, and without us writing about it, they wouldn't have gotten the information out to the public. It just grew out of itself."

Motor Trend was created soon after *Hot Rod* [in 1949], almost by accident. "As I went out to advertisers," Petersen recalled, "I was thrown out of a few offices. People said, 'I

Earlier in the year, Bill NieKamp's Ford Model A won the America's Most Beautiful Roadster trophy at the Oakland Roadster Show. He brought the 9-foot trophy home with him, displaying it here at the 1950 Motorama.

don't want to have my name associated with *Hot Rod*.' I had a long talk with [race car builder] Frank Kurtis. He said, 'If you do a magazine about something else and call it something else, I'd be in it and I'd buy an ad.' I had other people say that. At that time, Indianapolis [500] was the hot deal. The general public hated hot rods. So I said, 'Maybe we should get something for *that* market.' By now we had a way to do it, and we knew how to do it, so we brought in Walt Woron. He'd been writing for *Hot Rod*; he was from Lockheed and he was more of a sports car guy."

Soon there was competition. "*Speed Age* was already there," said Petersen. "*Car Life* would come out, but then it disappeared. Fawcett came out with a book called *Best Hot Rods*. They were going to publish out East, and we ate 'em up. They didn't know anything. A guy came in from Fawcett with a suit and the whole thing, and made a big pitch to Phil Weiand. I was there working on my roadster. Phil said, 'What do you think of all that?' And I said, 'I dunno. I think

that's a bunch of shit, Phil. I'd never buy that.' And the Fawcett guy said, 'Well, who're you?' And I said, 'I'm the publisher of *Hot Rod*.'"

Hot Rod's advertised circulation hit 500,000 by the April 1952 issue. That was a substantial number of people to be reading a magazine about an "outlaw" sport. Naturally, *HRM* spawned many imitators. By the early 1950s, most hot rod magazines cost a quarter apiece, about the same as a pack of cigarettes or a gallon of high-test gasoline. They came in two sizes: "big" (8 1/2x11) and "little" (5 1/2x8). Color pages were sparse at first. Technical tips and tantalizing speed equipment ads were plentiful. There were readers' car photos, pin-ups with Hollywood starlets holding manifolds and camshafts, great and not-so-great feature cars, hop-up equipment comparisons, and even road tests.

For youngsters across America, these magazines served as an open window to California, to the hallowed dry lakes, to Bonneville, and to rods and customs that were the stuff of their

The *Hot Rod* magazine Trophy is displayed in the So-Cal/Edelbrock booth at the 1950 Motorama. The Edelbrock-equipped So-Cal streamliner set fastest speed at Bonneville to win the trophy. The award is still presented every year at Speed Week. *Robert E. Petersen Collection*

In 1951, the Motorama was relocated to the Pan Pacific Auditorium. Dick Kraft's T roadster and Roy Desbrow's 1932 Ford pickup are seen with Sandy Belond's Miss Equa-Flow girl. Desbrow's truck was featured on *Hot Rod's* January 1952 cover; years later, Kraft's car resurfaced as the *Highland Plating Special* on HRM's March 1962 cover. *Robert E. Petersen Collection*

dreams. Packed with early hot rod lore, the oldies are much more fun today to read than more recent editions. Best of all, through thousands of faded pages, the entire panorama of hot rodding's peripatetic history unfolds. The word spread quickly. A kid in Des Moines or Indianapolis could see how the guys in California built their cars, and soon cars from all across the country began appearing, first in the "Mailbag" section, and then in features.

Hot Rod grew exponentially. The first standard-size issue, October 1949, saw Wally Parks as editor and John Bond (later editor of *Road & Track*) as a contributor. That issue covered the first Bonneville Nationals, too. "Parts with Appeal" featured actress Barbara Britten, and, for the first time, listed the model's bust, waist, and hip measurements. HRM's first color cover, on the April 1951 issue, proclaimed, "Drag Strips Develop Phenomenal Speeds." In May 1952, circulation of "American's How-To Magazine" topped the half-million mark. Five years later, *Hot Rod*, *Motor Trend*, and *Motor Life* boasted a combined circulation of 1.1 million.

Those early magazines tracked the development of the sport, bearing witness to the steady evolution of hot rods and customs, as well as recording racing action at the lakes, Bonneville, and the drags. Theirs was a wealth of firsthand reference material to aid anyone wanting to build a car, plus evocative ads like this one, copied from a September 1954, classified in *HRM*'s "Hot Rod Mart":

"SELL—'51 Barris Kustom Mercury, chopped and channeled, custom upholstery, plastic knobs, Chromed '53 Cad engine, featured in March '53 *MT* and *HRM*, $4900. B Hirohata, 9857 La Rosa Dr., Temple City, Calif., Madison 9-8451 or Atlantic 7-8605."

Now wouldn't you like to call for *that* car, today?

Indeed, there were countless examples of rodding ingenuity in each issue. Audacious

Like Robert E. Petersen, the man he worked for, Wally Parks, understood the value of promotion. And so when he was named the NHRA's first director he assumed his role with vigor. He's seen here stumping for the NHRA at the 1951 Motorama in Los Angeles. *Robert E. Petersen Collection*

The primary purpose of a hot rod is for driving. So said Bud Crackbon, owner of the 1952 America's Most Beautiful Roadster winner. He's seen here in his trophy hot rod during a roadside stop. *Mario Baffico Collection*

engine swaps, innovative induction systems, the steady recognition of hot, new models and power plants. And always, there was a relentless urge to do things better and more creatively than Detroit's automakers could.

During those days, Petersen Publishing raced from one success to another. "It was crazy," recalled Petersen. "In just a few years we were selling 85 to 90 percent [per issue] on the newsstands. At one time we were doing 375,000 on the stands . . . we were outselling *Time* magazine on newsstands. All this happened when we got a national distributor. That enabled us to come up with an idea [for a new book] and have it on the stands immediately. Then we started getting into this niche deal. We'd say, 'They need a magazine for custom cars, et cetera.' That's when we started splitting. In those days we didn't care that much about advertising. We made money on newsstands whenever we launched something good."

Hop Up, published by Enthusiast Publications out of Glendale, California, officially bowed in August 1951. (According to the late Dean Batchelor, who was *Hop Up*'s advertising manager, a limited-circulation July 1951 issue was printed first. When this looked to be successful, it was repeated as the nearly identical August 1951 issue. July copies are very rare.) *Hop Up* was actually a spin-off of *Road and Track* (later spelled *Road & Track*), ostensibly to compete with *Hot Rod*, but for a younger market.

Hop Up's first editor, Oliver Billingsley, explained in an editorial, "[W]e have had many requests to include material on other activities such as hot rods, custom cars . . . now we can cover those subjects without varying the policy of *Road and Track*." Recognizing that "many of *Hop Up*'s readers may be of a young age group, we have decided on a small page size and a fifteen-cent price." That explains the "little book" strategy that was later copied by *Rod & Custom*, *Honk!*, and *Car Craft*.

By April 1952, *Hop Up* had color covers (with Wally Welch's Gil Ayala–built chopped gold Mercury on that cover). The magazine went to a large format in March 1953 (to better compete against Petersen's *Hot Rod* and *Motor Trend*), but two issues later it was combined with *Motor Life* before being phased completely into *Motor Life* in 1959

The influence of track roadsters is seen on this car displayed at the 1952 Oakland Roadster Show. The nerf bar, split windshield, and flamed paint job were familiar features at roundy-round tracks of the time. *Mario Baffico Collection*

when Petersen Publishing bought it. There are wonderful color renderings in the large-size editions of *Hop Up*, plus great period photos by Jerry Cheseborough (who also shot for *Road & Track*) and Ralph Poole.

The first *Rod & Custom* appeared in May 1953. For that now-rare issue only, it was called *Rods and Customs*. *R&C* was a Quinn Publication, with Spence Murray as editor. According to Batchelor, "the first time Bob Petersen saw it was when someone put a copy on his desk." Petersen (who had just launched *Honk!* at the same time) recovered from his shock and bought *R&C* in July 1955. Early issues are laced with Roger Huntington's abstruse theories. (For example, limited by the tires and technology of the era, dragsters, he insisted, could never exceed 150 miles per hour.)

R&C had fascinating how-to articles featuring George Barris and other custom notables, and dramatic project car renderings by Ocee Rich. Readers all over the United States could follow the work, step-by-step, and modify their own cars. To counter Tom Medley's "Stroker McCurk" in *HRM*, *R&C* had its own cartoon character—a rodder named Arin Cee (get it?). The first full-size *Rod & Custom* appeared in August 1961.

R&C was folded into *Hot Rod* in June 1971 only to reappear intact in July 1972 (probably to battle Tom McMullen's *Street Rodder*, which debuted in May of that year, and *Rod Action*, which ex-Petersen staffer Ray Brock began in January of the previous year).

The San Francisco Ramblers were out in force for the 1952 Oakland Roadster Show. At lower left is Bud Crackbon's roadster pickup that took home the coveted AMBR trophy. Spectators could get up close and personal with the cars and their owners. *Mario Baffico Collection*

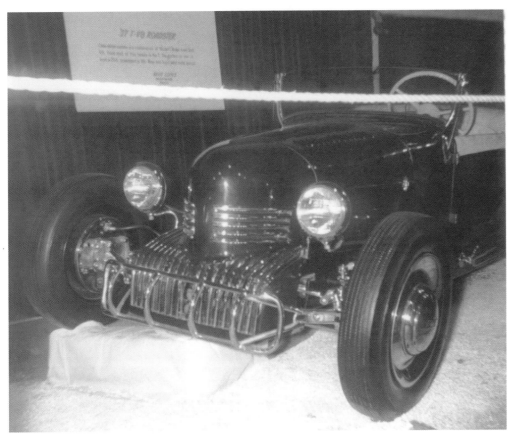

Some interesting designs evolved during the early car-show era. Mike Lopez's unique Model A–based street rod seen at the 1952 Los Angeles Motorama has a custom nose made from a 1939 Dodge, and a cowl section from a 1927 Model T. *Mario Baffico Collection*

What was it like to be an automotive photographer during the early years? Proof is in the pudding, so to speak, as *Hot Rod*'s most famous f-stop, Eric Rickman, is seen hard at work with his medium-format camera in hand at Bonneville. *Mario Baffico Collection*

Rod & Custom folded yet again, seemingly for all time, in May 1974. But Petersen Publishing resurrected it again in December 1988 under the tutelage of Pat Ganahl, and it continues to be published today. Obviously, those "Bring back *R&C* T-shirts" of the time worked! True collectors know there are gaps in the sequence so they don't hunt for issues that never appeared.

As noted earlier, another fine "little book," *Honk!*, appeared in May 1953, coincidentally with the first issue of *R&C*. The publisher was Robert Petersen, working under the banner Trend, Inc., *Honk!*'s initial focus was a mix of rods and customs. Wally Parks was the editorial director, and contributors included Ak Miller and John Christy. *Honk!* had several cartoon characters, including a Dennis the Menace–like kid named "Lil' Beep" and a custom counterpart of Stroker McGurk called "Honker." Both were drawn by Dick Day. Early issues of *Honk!*, all with color covers, sold for 25 cents.

In December 1953, *Honk!* was renamed *Car Craft*. There still remained a hot rod component to its editorial agenda, but the magazine's focus was clearly on custom cars. In 1961, it changed to a large-size format, and has remained so ever since. Today, *Car Craft* covers primarily late-model Pro-Street vehicles.

Sometimes, to get to the action, you need to be a part of the action. To that end the crew at *Hot Rod* magazine converted a '27 T on loan from Manny Ayulo into a camera car that took them onto the Bonneville Salt Flats for some interesting car-to-car shots. It was innovations like this that helped propel Petersen Publishing to the forefront of automotive journalism. *Mario Baffico Collection*

The hot rod and custom car craze spawned many competitors. Although *Road & Track* was ostensibly a sports car magazine, early issues included articles on road racers like Max Balchowski, whose Buick nailhead–powered Deuce roadster ran rings around imports and was the precursor of his *Old Yeller* specials. *Motor Trend* featured many rods and customs through its 1950s issues.

Speed Age, which began in May 1947, covered circle-track racing, new-model cars, and racing boats. In an effort to span the entire automotive gamut before more specialized books appeared, there was the occasional custom car or hot rod feature story.

There also were several Midwest and East Coast rod magazines by publishers like Fawcett, Ziff-Davis, Magnum, and Universal. Titles included *Car Speed & Style*, *Rodding & Re-styling*, *Speed Mechanics*, and *Rods Illustrated*. Each had its brief moment in the sun before fading into obscurity. As a general rule, their editorial matter, feature cars, and format were not quite up to the higher standards set by Petersen and Quinn publications.

Just as the magazines were highly competitive, so were the big car shows. It didn't take long after the 1948 SCTA effort at the L.A. Armory before several major competitive indoor hot rod shows sprang up in the Los Angeles area.

Among the early hot rod titles was *Hop Up* magazine. Don Ferrara's fenderless A-V8 roadster graced the cover of the November 1952 cover. Behind him is Norm Jennings' full-fendered roadster. *Hop Up* was discontinued, but has recently made a return and is published as a special once a year by Hop Up Products. *Don Ferrara Collection*

Bob Barsky, who'd worked with Petersen and the SCTA on that first Armory show (and who was one of the people objecting to Pete's bold new magazine), teamed up with Lou Baney and the Russetta Timing Association to produce a series of hot rod and motorsports shows from 1949 to 1952. Their program was primarily a directory of speed equipment manufacturers. Not to be outdone, Bob Petersen founded a series of Motorama Shows at L.A.'s Pan-Pacific Auditorium.

In 1949, Harold "Baggy" Bagdasarian started a small hot rod show in Sacramento that soon grew into a much larger event. And in Oakland, California, Al Slonaker's Oakland Roadster Show (soon to be called the Grand National Roadster Show) began in January 1950. The Michigan Hot Rod Association's still-extant Detroit Autorama started in 1952, and four years later, under the direction of professional promoter Don Ridler, it grew exponentially. Eventually, the Detroit Autorama fell under the auspices of the Michigan Hot Rod Association (MHRA) Raceway boss, Bob Larivee, who later developed the International Championship Auto Show Series (ICAS) and the Hot Rod/Custom Car World.

On the East Coast, beginning in 1951, Joe Kizis' Autoramas held in Springfield, Massachusetts; Hartford, Connecticut; and other cities combined hot rods and customs with new sports cars and passenger models. Event programs featured photographs of show cars, all their modifications, and even the cost of the work that was done.

But it was Bob Petersen's Los Angeles car show efforts that especially fostered a national trend. "When we started with the first show," Petersen recalled, "that spawned all the other hot rod and custom car shows. There'd never been another one before—we then went to Detroit and put on a big car show. Our idea was to bring in Detroit [industry] people to see what these cars looked like. We also did a big drag race in Detroit. We had all the heads of the car companies there."

The rationale for these exhibits was so people could actually *see* the cars; the shows enhanced the sport; they weren't a competitive venture. "We started doing events to bring

advertisers in to see our activities," Petersen recalled. "We went back East with Herb Shriner and we started the first auto show in New York after the war at the New York Armory. Herb had come to our L.A. Motorama, which we had begun doing after the first West Coast hot rod shows."

Ever the promoter, Petersen recalled: "When we started Motorama we said to Tony Nancy, 'Why don't we have you go down the street in your dragster and just rap your pipes a little bit. That'd be exciting for the guys going to the opening of the Motorama.' I talked to this police sergeant and asked if it would be OK if Tony 'just went down the street' and he said, 'Yeah, I'll clear the people out of the way.' Of course, Tony did a full burnout and went roaring down the goddamn street. He blew windows and light bulbs out of office buildings. I had to pay for it. But they'll always remember it.

Among the top show cars from the 1950s was the *Polynesian*, built for Jack Stewart by Neil Emory and Clay Jensen of Valley Customs. The car began life as a 1950 Oldsmobile and was known for the metalwork that Emory and Jensen performed on it. *Robert E. Petersen Collection*

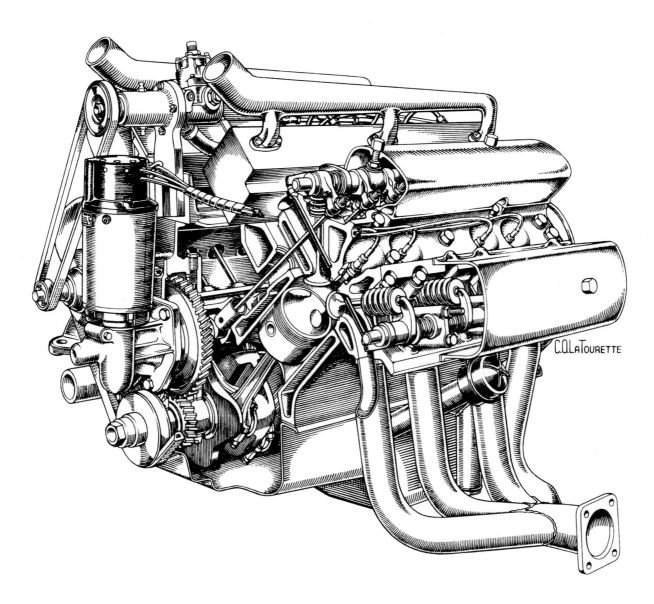

C.O.LaTourette

Hot rod magazines gave enthusiasts all the latest news and technical information. This cutaway drawing of C&T Automotive's radical DOHC engine that started life as a Ford flathead appeared in the March 1953 issue of *Hop Up*. Illustrator C. O. LaTourette is best known for his later work in *Sports Cars Illustrated* (now *Car & Driver*). *Jim Miller Collection*

"Our Motorama show did well [in Hollywood] for quite a while. I was trying to expand it, but General Motors [which had its own shows called GM Motoramas] and the local politicians wouldn't let me keep on going. I had 60,000 square feet right next to Graumann's Chinese Theatre. I owned the building and I still own it. We used the bottom part for the show. And we were going to move into the top part and do a whole rehab on it. But the city fathers said the upper floor wouldn't take the weight, so we finally had to give the Motorama up. Much later, we had the idea to do the Petersen Automotive Museum."

Reflecting about the early days of the magazines and the shows, Bob Petersen said, "I don't really think it's changed all that much. If I could take you back to the first hot rod show, I don't see that much difference, really. When you think about it, you had '32 Fords, you had T-buckets, you had all the same things then. They started putting race car noses on hot rods

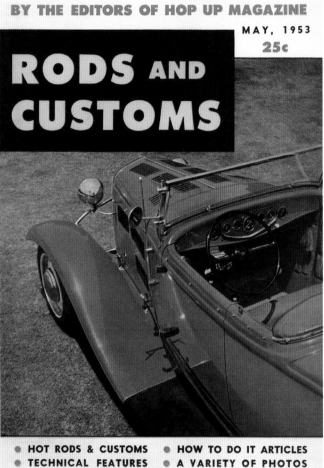

BY THE EDITORS OF HOP UP MAGAZINE

MAY, 1953

25¢

RODS AND CUSTOMS

- HOT RODS & CUSTOMS
- TECHNICAL FEATURES
- HOW TO DO IT ARTICLES
- A VARIETY OF PHOTOS

In 1956, Ollie Morris ran this Chevrolet-powered rear-engine drag-ster sponsored by Offenhauser Equipment Company. Morris later worked for Offenhauser, helping develop intake manifolds such as the Dual Plane 360. *Fred and Mary Lou Larsen Collection*

and that became a big deal. I remember I was so excited when I saw the first guy who did it, but guys are still doin' it now and it's still exciting.

"These new people are grinding a lot of stuff out," Petersen added. "I started *Hot Rod* and *Motor Trend* television shows. In fact, I did the first hot rod show that was ever done on televi-sion on KTLA in Los Angeles. We'd have the cars drive into the alley; we only had one camera, and we'd talk to the drivers. Roy Maple was my emcee and that was the first car show on TV I'd heard of. Then we had big TV coverage of our Motoramas. I remember once Ab Jenkins was there with his *Mormon Meteor*. It had a rollback canopy over the driver. The announcer said, 'Tell us all about the *Mormon Meteor*, Ab.' Ab said, 'Would you like to sit in there?' So the announcer got inside and Ab just shut the canopy up, left the guy inside, and went on talking."

While it lasted, the early hot rod and custom show car era produced some truly wild-looking automobiles. In hindsight, the earliest customs are arguably the purest in concept, relying on extensive metalwork and selective use of borrowed items like grilles, side trim, hubcaps, and head-lamps from more expensive donor cars of the period to alter and streamline their appearance. The second phase of the custom era, when bulbous '49 to '51 Mercury coupes and convertibles were transformed into sleek, almost sinister creations, caught the attention of the automakers.

continued on page 124

Quinn Publishing, operating out of Glendale, California, joined the hot rod ranks in 1953 with *Rods and Customs* magazine. Volume 1, Number 2 hit the newsstands as *Rod & Custom*, as it remains today. The maga-zine's first cover car was a 1932 Ford roadster belonging to Chuck Price of Alhambra, California. *Jim Miller Collection*

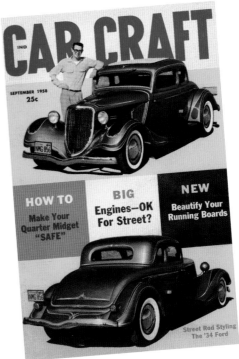

Car Craft's September 1958 cover featured the chopped and sectioned 1934 Ford belonging to Ted Svendsen of San Diego, California. The five-window was powered by a Ford 292 Y-block that Svendsen pirated from a Thunderbird. *Jim Miller Collection*

Norm Grabowski's Cadillac-powered T-bucket set a styling trend that remains today. The car is sometimes referred to as the *Kookie Car* because it was driven by the character Kookie on the TV series *77 Sunset Strip. Fred and Mary Lou Larsen Collection*

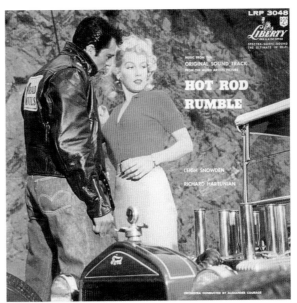

Here's one way to set a record without even firing up the engine! Tommy Ivo's famous T-bucket helped create the setting on the album jacket for the original soundtrack recording to the 1957 Allied Artists' movie *Hot Rod Rumble. Tommy Ivo Collection*

By the early 1960s, custom car shows were popular all across the country. This bubble-top Corvette is among the many cars displayed at a show held in the Civic Center at Long Beach, California. *Robert E. Petersen Collection*

A car show in the 1960s wasn't complete unless it had a star attraction. One of the top marquee names was Ed Roth, who built some wild-looking cars. This is the *Outlaw* at the Great Western Rod & Custom Show, January 1960. *Fred and Mary Lou Larsen Collection*

continued from page 119

Hot rods and custom cars began to fall out of favor when the Detroit manufacturers began building new models that adopted many of the styling features that customizers had already popularized. The top custom builders, primarily from California but including Detroit's own "A Brothers," Mike and Larry Alexander, were invited to Detroit by some of the automakers as styling advisors. Further mimicking the custom car crowd, Ford Motor Company held its own custom car show in 1955 at the Ford Rotunda in Dearborn.

By the mid-1960s, influenced by the custom crowd, simple dechroming and lowering were still popular, but the overall lines of new models were so clean that very little bodywork was needed to make them look better. Detroit engineers, having learned their hot rod lessons, were dropping big V-8 engines into lighter cars, creating street screamers like the Pontiac GTO—the cars now known as muscle cars.

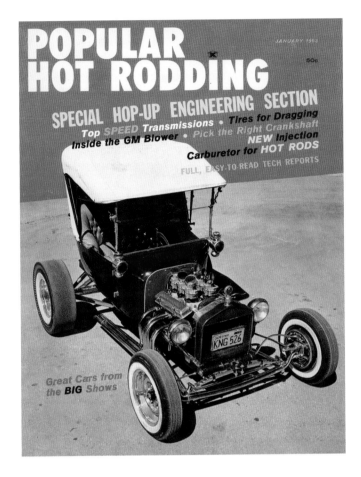

Perhaps the best, and most respected, non–Petersen Publishing hot rod publication was *Popular Hot Rodding,* first published in 1962. The cover car for the January 1963 issue was Gary Hendrickson's T-bucket, powered by a Corvette small-block fed by six deuces. *Jim Miller Collection*

Hot Rod magazine was the genre's leading publication, but other titles continually came and went as hot rodding evolved and grew. Among them was *Cars,* published in New York City. The July 1963 cover featured Vic Zaikine's heavily customized 1955 Mercury. *Jim Miller Collection*

By the mid-'60s the muscle car era was well under way. The car's engine and its output became the most important feature. Radical body modifications were no longer popular—except among a small coterie of diehards—although scalloped paint and exterior trim modifications kept restyling alive until the early 1970s. Then, accelerated by the energy crisis and rising environmental concerns, hot rodding went into hibernation.

The sport enjoyed a renaissance in the late 1980s and it's alive and thriving today. *Hot Rod, Street Rodder,* and a score of rivals remain popular and influential among enthusiasts. A variation of the old Oakland Roadster Show (now called the San Francisco Rod, Custom and Motorcycle Show), the Grand National Roadster Show (now located in Pomona, California), and the Detroit Autorama are bigger than ever. Looking back, the growth of this exciting and vibrant sport grew exponentially thanks to the early enthusiast magazines and custom car shows.

CHAPTER 6

FROM OUT OF THE EAST . . .

If someone builds a hot rod and nobody writes about it, does it exist?

By A. B. Shuman

THEY BEGAN APPEARING IN THE LATE 1990S: books, DVDs, and Web pages about postwar hot rodding taking place "back East." That is to say, outside of Southern California. Fueled by nostalgia, they tell the stories the mainstream hot rod publications of the 1950s didn't. Books of this previously overlooked genre aren't merely the equivalents of smeary VHS re-dubs of faded home movies set to rock 'n' roll soundtracks, but seriously researched works. There's a lot of setting the record straight in them, too.

Much of the apparent provincialism of early West Coast rodding magazines can be linked to their beginnings as dry lakes racing chronicles. But, according to Dean Batchelor in his book, *The American Hot Rod*, *Hot Rod* magazine was meant to be a national publication right from its start in 1948. Still, the coverage of cars beyond California's Los Angeles, Ventura, Riverside, and Orange counties was painfully sparse. And, when non-California cars were featured, they seemed to be posited as chance points of light in a black sky. Generally, there wasn't a feeling a local hot rod culture existed.

Bill Shikrallah signs off on a channeled '32 Ford five-window from Massachusetts, and signals the tech crew to shoe-polish the number and class onto the car's door. Like most street-driven hot rod coupes, this car ran in an altered class. *Carl Debien Collection*

Though a continent away from California's dry lakes racing scene, New England drag racers were influenced by the cars they saw in *Hot Rod* magazine. This street-legal flathead-powered '34 three-window had small wings alongside its speedway-inspired nose. *A. B. Shuman*

It's not that hot rodding had no real pre-'50s basis in the eastern half of the country. Buckboard-like Model T speedsters of the teens and '20s (themselves inspired by the factory hot rod Stutz Blackhawks built in Indianapolis, and Mercer Raceabouts from Trenton, New Jersey) often got their go from speed parts built in the Midwest. Most rodders know the Ardun (from "ARkus-DUNtov") overhead-valve, hemi-head conversion for the Ford flathead was designed by Zora Arkus-Duntov and his brother in New York in the late '40s (well before Zora became the patriarch of the Corvette, or Chevy parts departments offered Duntov cams). Three decades before the Ardun, though, in Anderson, Indiana, Robert Roof began producing one of America's first pieces of serious speed equipment: a 16-valve racing head for the Model T. A later version designed expressly for street use came in 1919. Early advertising for Roof showed several fenderless, teardrop-bodied T roadsters—hot rods—in front of Roof's Indiana shop.

Indiana was also home to the Chevrolet brothers, whose approach to souping the Ford Model T engine was a total package, from flywheel to magneto, topped with their own Frontenac rocker-arm head. The equally famous RaJo head for the T was produced in Racine,

Wisconsin. These and similar "pieces from the East" helped propel many of the top Southern California dry lakes race cars during the '30s. Even in the twenty-first century, avidly watching fast four-bangers at NHRA events, Wally Parks remained a fan, pointing out, "This is where it started!"

When *Hot Rod* announced the formation of "a national hot rod association" in its May 1951 issue, it was an affirmation that the pastime was not merely a regional oddity. The following issue carried the names of the first 50 people to join the newborn National Hot Rod Association. Only 11 had California addresses, while two dozen lived in states east of the Mississippi. The July issue listed an additional 350 charter members, the vast preponderance from the East. Still, editorial coverage of hot rod events outside of California lagged in *Hot Rod* and other magazines.

Yet, all over the country, returning war veterans and teenage *Hot Rod* readers were building and modifying cars, joining clubs, and (after ordering jackets, plaques, and courtesy cards) battling to establish local drag strips. That was exactly what was happening, for example, in New England, clean across the continent from L.A.

A quick-change rear end was too expensive for Herb Dreher, so the Hingham, Massachusetts, hot rodder alternated between two rear-axle assemblies for his Model A. For daily driving chores he used a third-member with a numerically low ratio. A set with a numerically high ratio served its worth at the drag strip on weekends. *A. B. Shuman*

Kenny Hodges originally built this channeled '32 Ford coupe in 1952–1953. For power, it had a tri-carb flathead V-8 from a '52 Mercury. Ty-Rod car club member Frank Domenichella owned the car for more than 50 years before letting it slip away. It was last seen in South Carolina. *A. B. Shuman*

New England, like other parts of the country, developed its own style of hot rod. In a word, it was *low*. From about 1951, the New England trend toward channeled cars was in full swing. By 1955 virtually all early-'30s-bodied hot rods—including some stock-fendered ones—had their bodies dropped over the frame. Channeled roadsters and convertibles commonly had chopped windshields, too, but closed cars were almost always uncut. A number of the cars had a unique front face: '30s-vintage Ford pickup truck grilles were commonly seen on '32 to '34 models, with varying visual results. Many trace it to a specific black '32 roadster: New England oldsters call it "the Bannister car," and it hit the streets in Massachusetts in 1949.

Front cycle fenders, with very few exceptions, were also the rule. At the rear, either cycle fenders or heavily bobbed stock types were usually fitted. Only a few dared to routinely drive bare-tire cars. This was not merely due to often-sloppy weather—there were stringent state safety inspections coupled with punishing anti–hot rod law enforcement to contend with. In Massachusetts, things automotive were administrated by the Registry of Motor Vehicles, which had its own police arm. "Registry cops" roamed the Bay State's roads (it seemed too often), waiting only for a chance to pounce on some hapless hot rodder. These unkindly folk had the power to conduct vehicle inspections if they just suspected a car to be out of compliance. In one case, a car that met all state requirements during a roadside stop was ordered driven to a service station, where a cylinder head was pulled. Measurement of the bore showed it was larger than stock. Since the road tax was based on a simple formula using bore diameter, the rodder was given a ticket for . . . tax evasion.

The vitality of New England activity was pointed out dramatically in *Hot Rod*'s report on the 1955 NHRA "Safari" drag meet in Orange, Massachusetts. It carried the surprising observation that "this general area now leads California in the number of on-the-street hot rods—good equipment too." When this was written, there was a boom in the formation of hot rod clubs in the area. But it all started with a few individuals who served as nodes in what was to become a thriving hot rod/drag racing culture.

continued on page 135

The En Regle Club of Dedham, Massachusetts, held an annual car show in mid-summer. This bronze-colored Model T debuted at the 1958 event. The roadster had a large-diameter tube frame with four-bar linkage. Inspired by dry lakes modifieds, it carried a '27 T touring front body section with a '37 pickup grille and a flathead V-8 for power. *A. B. Shuman*

This clean '32 Ford three-window was built by No-Mads car club member George Karalekis. The "R" on the license plate stands for "Repair," meaning that the car needs further work before it can be officially licensed. The body sat so low that the door bottoms were trimmed to swing open over the side pipes. *A. B. Shuman*

Murray Kidder's low-slung coupe first hit the drag strips in 1956. The car is seen here on a trailer before being unloaded at the Orange drags. The Model A had a flathead V-8 tucked inside the body, and the driver sat in what was the originally cowl section. *A. B. Shuman*

Eventually, the engine in Kidder's coupe made way for a Chevy small-block, and a bullet nose was added for streamlining. In turn, the Chevy engine was replaced with a more powerful Cadillac V-8. The bodywork included masking tape over the rear windows! *A. B. Shuman*

As Murray Kidder's Model A coupe progressed at the drag strip, his younger brother, Bruce, became its driver. By now the outfit was known as the 99 Racing Team. Bill Peterson, who later became the team's driver, was notoriously nervous before running, but always did a great job. *A. B. Shuman*

George Miller was among the East Coast's first successful drag racers. His chopped and channeled '33 Ford coupe qualified to race at the NHRA Nationals at Great Bend, Kansas. Miller learned much from his trip to Kansas. One lesson was to replace the old flathead with a 392-cubic-inch Chrysler Hemi. *A. B. Shuman*

George Miller reviews the tech inspection sheet prior to having his car inspected for the Orange drags. When the NHRA's Safety Safari team made its national tour in 1954, hot rod clubs across the country gained a better understanding of safety and build techniques. *A. B. Shuman*

continued from page 131

In Massachusetts, a quintet of men—Fran Bannister and "Mudd" Sharrigan, their younger brothers, Ralph Bannister and John Sharrigan, and Michael Hartney—in their twenties helped form the core of the New England hot rod movement from the late '40s through the mid-'50s. Fran Bannister had picked up his addiction in the army during World War II while stationed in Northern California and inculcated its purest precepts to Ralph. Mudd Sharrigan learned about hot rods from shipmates' snapshots in the merchant marine, and would, like the Bannisters, contribute to New England's movement to channeled cars, building one of the first. (At the time, the "technology" was so new he wrote to *Hot Rod* asking what to do for a floor.)

John Sharrigan, known to most as "Shag," became the most colorful—some would say outrageous—personality on the scene and one of the area's most multitalented drivers, setting records in everything from fuel dragsters on airport strips to skeleton sleds on Monte Carlo's icy 'n' dicey Cresta Run. Off the track, he was both a pragmatic craftsman and a lover of practical jokes, particularly ones involving loud explosives. His mustachioed and goateed face became a symbol of the hard-partying, hard-racing No-Mads of Newton (Massachusetts).

What might appear to be a sprint car is Dave Watson's ice racer from New Hampshire, seen here in the pits at Sanford. The four-man crew is preparing to lift the engine out of the frame so they can replace the clutch disk. *A. B. Shuman*

The Minch brothers' 1928 Ford roadster pickup from New York looked ready to race in June 1958, but it stayed in the spectator parking lot at Sanford. The little truck had a Corvette engine with four carburetors and a Vertex magneto ignition. The roll bar was shaped from cut and welded tube sections. *A. B. Shuman*

John "Shag" Sharrigan was literally the face of the No-Mads—his likeness was on the club's plaque and on the side of their first dragster, a belly tank–inspired affair dubbed the *Bubblegum Special* because its thin aluminum body panels were as wrinkled as an old gum wrapper. He set a Sanford strip record of 144 miles per hour with this nitro-fed, four-carb, Chrysler-powered dragster. *A. B. Shuman*

Hartney, universally known as "Jack," was from rural Orange, Massachusetts, and had no inkling of hot rodding when he bought his '32 roadster weeks before his sixteenth birthday—and shortly before the attack on Pearl Harbor. He enlisted in the navy soon thereafter by lying about his age. The first hot rod he saw was a channeled Deuce roadster, "like mine, but lower, much lower," he recalls, adding, "I fell in love with the fenderless look." That hot rod was parked in front of a bar in Tarzana, California, where jazz singer Mel Torme was performing in 1943. It was what Torme drove to the gig. Hartney (NHRA charter member 88) built his hot rod fenderless, but not channeled (to preserve legroom), a few years after he returned home. Painted a lavender hue, it was powered by a 296-cubic-inch V-8 flathead. He became a key player in helping establish New England's longest-lived airport-based drag strip, in Orange, operating from 1954 through 1970.

After the war, the Bannister brothers worked as machinists and mechanics for a Boston trucking company and had the know-how and tools to build just about anything connected with hot rods or racing. As Ralph said years later, "What we didn't have, we made." His son

Ron Carson was only 16 years old when he chopped and channeled this '32 Ford three-window. He lowered the car a total of 11 inches from its stock height and painted it 1955 Ford Tropical Rose "'cause no one else had one that color." *A. B. Shuman*

Steven has expanded, telling of their weekly trips to the town dump: "We usually brought back more than what we left." As illustration, in the mid-'50s the brothers built a blown flathead dragster that was dominant well into the era of overheads. Its V-belt and magneto drives were homemade, while its 4-71 supercharger was scavenged from a burned-out bus.

Fran's daily driver in 1947 was a stock-appearing '32 coupe with a horizontal McCullough blower atop its rebuilt flathead. The only external giveaway was a "Supercharged" emblem. Harley rider Don Gale noticed that emblem one day as he sized up the coupe at a stoplight. A few seconds later, Fran left him at the green. It took 2 miles to catch up, but Gale finally got Bannister to pull into a gas station and open the hood, telling him he'd "never been beaten by a Ford." The two became friends, and Fran helped Don build a '32 highboy roadster. Gale was a long-haul trucker, and when he began to get more cross-country jobs, he decided to sell his car to Fran. This was to become Bannister's unique channeled street roadster. Finished in 1949, its signature piece—a chromed, lightly chopped '39 pickup grille—was Ralph's idea. "I wanted the hood to have rounded side panels," he explained, adding that he formed them with his bare hands. The look was polarizing, but many picked up on that pickup truck part.

As built by Gale, the highboy roadster was fitted with Evans and Thickstun equipment. Though from California, Gale's source was Andy Granatelli's Chicago mail-order speed shop. Within a few years, however, there would be local sources for speed parts.

In the Boston area, Ed Stone—an early sponsor of midgets, stockers, and at least one drag car—was among the first to go beyond "chrome goodies" into actual "go fast" equipment. His

New England Auto Racing Equipment moved downtown to become New England Speed Equipment by 1953. Hub Auto, which did a heavy business in chrome accessories and basic bolt-ons, often hired popular local circle-track drivers as countermen. The operations were located near one another on Commonwealth Avenue, a main Boston thoroughfare, only intensifying their competition.

In Rhode Island, Sam Packard opened speed shops in Providence and Pawtucket. A successful midget driver (Ed Stone had sponsored one of his cars, incidentally) and an even more successful stock car racer, Packard would be the last surviving member of the group that formed NASCAR at Daytona's Streamline Hotel in 1947. He also participated at the drags, in the "Hot Rod Girl" roadster, an Olds-powered Deuce that was featured in the movie of that name in 1956. Packard was effectively retracing the route of another Rhode Island–based midget driver. In 1949, Ray Jannelle purchased a roadster built for Grant Piston Rings in California, running it at Bonneville and Daytona on his long way home to Pawtucket. The channeled Deuce's chief distinctions were a curved, one-piece Plexiglas windshield and a custom fabric top with twin oval rear windows.

As an aside, midget car racing was extremely popular in New England from the '30s to late '40s. A young fan who got hooked on his first exposure was Marvin Rifchin, who worked for his father, Harry, in a small car repair and tire business in Watertown, Massachusetts. Subsequent races and a ride in a midget when he was 15 convinced him that there was a need for better tires. He enlisted his father as a silent partner to subsidize the venture, and started a race tire recapping company called M&H in 1931. Much later, when midgets were replaced

Ted Wingate's channeled road-ster led a rather colorful life. After he and his brother Bob moved to California, their hot rods shared space on a *Hot Rod* cover. Later, Wingate replaced the flathead V-8 with a Buick nailhead V-8, and the folks at Mattel patterned one of their Hot Wheels toys after the car. *A. B. Shuman*

This deeply channeled Ford pickup carried its Buick V-8 and Dynaflow transmission behind a '32 Ford grille. The front nerf bars were ingeniously fabricated from a pair of bicy-cle handlebars. *A. B. Shuman*

Sanford capped its 1960 season with the Dave Sanderson Memorial Meet, benefiting the widow of a popular New Hampshire driver who drowned in a boating accident. On hand were pro drivers from the West, Chris "The Greek" Karamesines with his Top Fuel dragster, *Chizler*, and Lyle Fisher in the mid-engine *Speed Sport Special II*. *Bernie Shuman*

(Below left) Gene Lade's channeled '32 Ford three-window is considered one of New England's ageless hot rods. Shown here with a Ford flathead V-8 during a custom car show, the coupe later used a Cadillac OHV V-8 for some quick times at the drag strip. *George Miller*

(Left) This membership card says that Ron Carson is a member in good standing with the Piston Manglers for the year 1955. Carson learned about hot rods at an early age, constructing his first—a channeled '32 Ford three-window coupe—when he was 17 years old. *Ron Carson Collection*

in popularity by stock cars, M&H established its reputation as a top tire provider. Some of the early New England drag cars even ran M&H Racemasters (a name suggested by Ed Stone) designed for stock cars, but Rifchin wasn't aware of this—he didn't know about drag racing until the late '50s. He proved to be a quick learner, however, and M&H slicks succeeded in setting the standard for many years to come.

Other New Englanders were just as quick to learn about this new form of racing. Dick Morse, of the Dedham (Massachusetts) En Regle club, for example, used a stock '39 unit on his channeled '33 five-window coupe (which would later become the LaJoie & Redding *Blue Bird* altered, albeit with a '37 DeSoto nose) to get acquainted with drag racing. Another Massachusetts car, *The Owl*, built on Cape Cod in 1950, also featured a '39 pickup grille, but chopped to a near circle.

A member from each
participating club at the Dave
Sanderson Memorial Meet
posed for *Hot Rod*'s photographer, there to cover the meet.
The variety of club jackets is
proof of the enthusiasm among
East Coast rodders back in
the '50s and early '60s.
A. B. Shuman

Another alternative to the classic '32 Ford grille shell was the '37 truck grille shell, used to its greatest aesthetic advantage on Paul FitzGerald's channeled Deuce roadster, another early '50s car, since reconstructed by FitzGerald from many of its original parts. Sabie Rubbo's channeled '36 roadster was another car with a '37 truck grille. Up front, the hood was extended to meet the stock '37 shell. With snap-latches and leather hood straps, it had a taut look, as if the panels were trying to restrain a locomotive engine. Not everybody's cup of tea, but Rubbo is said to have driven it 400,000 miles. Friend Lenny Biondo now owns it.

Other, more conventional-looking cars with '37 grilles were Ty-Rods member Dick Kelly's channeled '33 three-window coupe, which he called *The Merger* after adding a small-block Chevy, and Frank Harlow's flathead-powered, homebuilt roadster that was styled like a classic British sports car. Kelly and Dick Morse were among the region's earliest adopters of Chevy V-8 power.

While working on Fran's roadster, Ralph Bannister started building his own car, a '39 coupe channeled 9 1/2 inches. At this point, Fran was concentrating on engine building and Ralph on fabrication. Their primary interest was in circle-track racing. Fran's '32 coupe had, in fact, set a track record at Lonsdale, Rhode Island, during the first NASCAR-sanctioned event there, but it was quickly disallowed because of the supercharger. By the end of the '40s,

the brothers saw oval-track stockers becoming evermore expensive so they turned their atten-tion to drag racing, helping to form the New England Timing Association (NETA).

NETA came into being in early 1950. Membership included sports car enthusiasts and hot rodders, most of them former GIs from the greater Boston area. The group (whose rac-ing rules generally followed SCTA's) began holding what were to become monthly "accelera-tion runs," starting that June. Each run yielded elapsed times for the standing quarter-mile, half-mile, and kilometer. The initial site was the municipal airport in Beverly, Massachusetts. Since the facility was in use by airplanes, there were stringent restrictions to prevent interfer-ence with the flyers. That meant NETA had to set up at about 6:00 a.m. and finish the racing before 8:30, even though they ran on an inactive runway. Some pilots objected, but it worked for two meets before a group of motorcyclists showed up and ran on another inactive run-way, prompting airport officials to cancel all racing.

Acting on a suggestion, Fran and Fred Cain, a teenage neighbor, drove their hot rods to Sanford, Maine, to try to wangle use of the former military airfield as a replacement for Beverly. Surprising themselves, they managed to convince the airport manager to let NETA run there. That handled and having successfully made the 190-mile round-trip, Fran, with his wife and infant child in the car, drove his roadster to Bonneville to run on the salt flats. Cain

Many local enthusiasts consider July 18, 1954, the date of origin for New England drag racing. That's when the airport drag strip in Orange, Massachusetts, sanctioned its first meet. There had been organized drag racing as early as 1950 in the area, but not for a sustained period in the same locale. *Carl Debien Collection*

(who would later become a successful, performance-oriented Chrysler dealer in Wilmington, Massachusetts) followed in their draft in a '39 Ford sedan. On the floor behind the driver's seat was a spare engine; tied to the roof and wrapped in canvas was a pipe tripod to swap it. Neither was needed. After only a change of carbs—suggested by Wally Parks—Bannister topped 127 miles per hour with his stock-stroke 258-inch flathead, respectable for this combo even today. Fran's roadster, having proved worthy, was later featured in *Hot Rod*.

The following year, another NETA car, the pretty Wentworth & Hoyt '32 highboy roadster from Peabody, Massachusetts, ran 129.9 miles per hour at Bonneville. Back at Sanford, Harvey Thomasian, driving his channeled '32 roadster, was the group's '51 champion, aided by a nonlinear throttle linkage he devised to minimize wheel spin on starts. (Thomasian later became an engineer; his GPA just missed the entrance cutoff, but he gained admission to Boston's Stevens Institute on the strength of building that car. Later, Paul FitzGerald, who drove his roadster to his admissions interview at Yale—a likely first—had an eerily similar experience in gaining acceptance as an engineering student. "My high school grades were good, but not all A's. The roadster was the clincher," he says.)

Jack Hartney was another early NETA member. He had sought out Fran Bannister after seeing his name in the *SCTA News*. (Their friendship endured, and he provided his roadster for Bannister to run at Bonneville at three meets in the late '80s.) Hartney and the Piston Manglers club led a determined years-long fight against the Massachusetts Department of Public Safety to establish a drag strip for hot rodders. The department was steadfastly opposed to allowing any form of drag racing in the Commonwealth. Finally, approval came in July 1954, although the Orange airport meets were labeled as "hot rod acceleration trials." The trials, held once a month, were sanctioned by the state government–endorsed Massachusetts Automotive Council. With the original NETA essentially moribund, MAC was allowed to assume the New England Timing Association name the following season.

NETA members Frank Harlow and Hal Stetson built and operated the area's first timing system, which was used at Orange. In an era before light beams triggered drag-strip timers,

The Strokers' *Sputnik*, with Carl Debien at the controls, was instantly outmoded in 1958 when the No-Mads' *Mirror Glaze Spl.* showed up at Charlestown. John Sharrigan, driving the No-Mads' car, set a low E.T. of 9.18 seconds for gas dragsters. The Strokers later resumed their winning ways with a blown Chrysler in a Scotty Fenn chassis. *Carl Debien Collection*

(Opposite page) Ed Sarkisian, SNETA's (Southern New England Timing Association) beloved PR guy and author of some 200 magazine articles about New England hot rodding, tactfully waits in victory circle at the Charlestown, Rhode Island, drag strip while the Debiens—Carl, winner of top eliminator, with wife Joan, the Powder Puff winner—"congratulate" each other. *Carl Debien Collection*

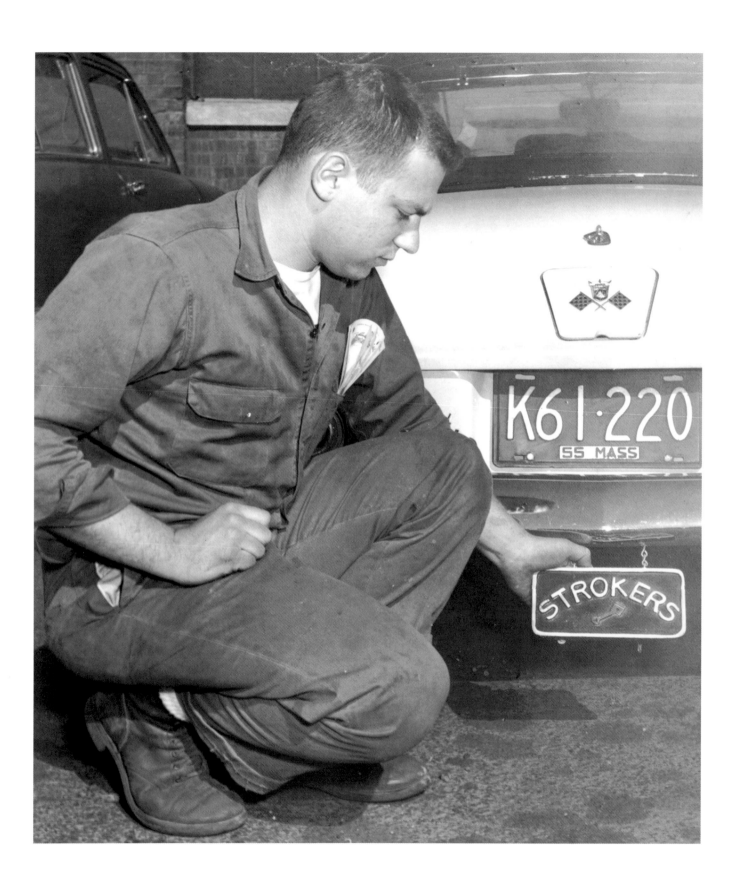

the Harlow-Stetson system used what amounted to a gas station hose to start the clock. Placed on what looked like a flattened hockey stick, the hose was placed by the starter on the ground just ahead of a front wheel. Meanwhile, Frank and Hal were on each end of the finish line, manning the timer for each lane. Scary, but NHRA was so impressed with their timer at the "Safari" race in 1955, they asked that the weighty system be lugged to Great Bend, Kansas, for the first Nationals.

In Connecticut, roadster owners Alan Wheeler, of Stratford, and William Purcella, of Derby, were leaders of the Bridgeport-based Southern Connecticut Auto Timing Society, or SCATS (an acronym cleverly close to SCTA), which existed at least from 1950 through 1953. According to old auto show programs, member cars were an eclectic mix of fendered and fenderless highboys and channeled rods (both Wheeler and Purcella had gone the channeled route by '53). Organized drag racing was the club's main focus. Frank Renzulli, running a '31 A-V8 roadster, was their 1950 champ.

The next year, in an attempt to establish region-wide cooperation to further hot rodding, SCATS convened a meeting that drew about 250 New England hot rodders from five of the six states. A report in *Hot Rod* touted that "Predictions (by whom, it's not clear) are that another five years will put the Conn.-Mass. sector on a par with the west coast." But SCATS would fade out of sight before the five years were up and long before the state got its first permanent drag strip: Frank Maratta's purpose-built Connecticut Dragway (1961).

In the early to mid-'50s, however, the greatest hot rod activity in the Nutmeg State centered around Joe Kizis' annual Autorama at the Hartford Armory. From its inception in

In the days before infrared beams and staging lights, an air hose tripped the timing clocks at the Orange drag strip. It took a very brave guy to hold the hose when cars like Walt Black's Corvette-powered coupe were set to launch. *Carl Debien Collection*

(Opposite page) Before Bob Tarozzi established his reputation by building fuel-burning Hemi engines for Keith Black and Brad Anderson, he served as a line mechanic at a Ford dealership in Springfield, Massachusetts. As a member of the Strokers, he raced a Thunderbird at the Orange drag strip. *Carl Debien Collection*

Despite its basic design, the Strokers' dragster was a dominant car in New England. Several members drove it initially, but Carl Debien soon became the full-time shoe. Debien (in T-shirt) poses with a fellow Strokers member with some of the trophies. Deb's speed shop had the advantage of a chassis dyno. *Carl Debien Collection*

1951, the Autorama included hot rods. Their participation quickly grew and the winter event soon became the largest hot rod and custom show in New England, even drawing cars from beyond the six-state region. In an era when heated garages were a rarity, meaning most shop work was confined to small projects in the basement, the February date made it the high point of the off-season. Among the out-of-area cars drawing most attention were Bill Neumann's $4,600 Model A roadster and Andy Kassa's asymmetrical *Cyclops* coupe, with custom nose by George Barris.

One standout Connecticut car at the '53 Autorama was Al Quagliaroli's '27 track roadster, for many years the only hot rod Model T in the show. "Don" Gallant (not his real name, as his license was suspended so many times he had to change it to get a new one) bought the car, and over the years powered it with 13 different engines. Some proved fast: At one meet, he says, the car hit the trifecta, setting low elapsed time and top speed and winning Top

Eliminator. Gallant was also the proprietor of one of Connecticut's first speed shops, Don's Automotive Specialties in Newington.

Predating the founding of NHRA by a few months, a small group in Rhode Island, headed by Bob Savory of Apponaug, formed SNETA, the Southern New England Timing Association, in January 1951. Its main purpose was to set up and operate a drag strip. It took until September 1956 to arrange two trial meets on one of the wide runways at the Navy Auxiliary Landing Field in Charlestown. The trials went well, and racing continued there until 1964. It helped that a share of the proceeds from each monthly meet went to the Navy Relief charity. Literally at the water's edge, yielding built-in barometric pressure advantages, the NHRA-sanctioned strip was run in an easygoing manner and, for competitors, was the site of some of the most enjoyable racing of the period.

Hot Rod magazine was NHRA's promotional handmaiden in its early days, and Wally Parks headed up both, ever on the hunt for stories to help build the organization's membership.

This front view of the Strokers' Scott Fenn chassis shows the rail dragster's unusual front axle treatment. A single rubber biscuit served as the front suspension. Clearly, the 1950s were pioneering times for this fledging sport. *Carl Debien Collection*

During a meet in 1959 at the Charlestown, Rhode Island, drag strip, Carl Debien wanted to experience a wheelie in the Strokers' new rail dragster. With the help of another club member tugging on the roll-bar cross-brace, Debien got his wheelie, although the front axle snapped upon landing. *Carl Debien Collection*

Among the mementos that George Miller brought back from the 1955 NHRA Nationals at Great Bend, Kansas, was this Participant's Permit. Rain on the final day postponed the race, which was later held in Arizona to determine class champions. *George Miller*

For instance, *Hot Rod*'s February 1953 issue reprinted a local newspaper article reporting the March 1952 formation of the Cam Snappers hot rod club in Newburyport, Massachusetts. The club's charter followed the NHRA template right down to having the town's police chief pose with the young members for a newspaper photo. Right after the issue hit Northeast mailboxes that January, three other New England clubs—and "a high-school kid"—contacted 19-year-old Jerry Sheehan, president of the Cam Snappers and de facto organizational guru. The kid was Dick Pratt, and he was in the midst of forming the No-Mads, which Ed Eaton would later liken to the fabled Bean Bandits of San Diego. Sheehan was present at its official founding at the local police station. Mudd Sharrigan was the president.

In 1953, the Cam Snappers and No-Mads, along with the Torque Masters (Rochester, New Hampshire); Ty-Rods (which had just broken away from the street-racing Piston Pushers) of Concord, Massachusetts; and Lords (Lowell, Massachusetts) formed the New England Hot Rod Council (NEHRC) with Sheehan as president. The raison d'etre for this club-only organization (it had no individual members) was to find a permanent place to drag race. More clubs joined, primarily from Massachusetts, but the local anti–hot rod sentiments meant the search was for a location elsewhere. There was a trio of practice races in New Hampshire, two at Newington in 1953, and one at Laconia the following year. Mudd Sharrigan stripped 400 pounds

PARTICIPANT'S PERMIT

1955 NATIONAL CHAMPIONSHIP DRAGS

sponsored by

NATIONAL HOT ROD ASSOCIATION

This permit entitles holder to purchase $.50 admission tickets.

NON-TRANSFERABLE

| Thurs., Sept. 29 | Fri., Sept. 30 | Sat., Oct. 1 | Sun., Oct. 2 |

Don Noyes' A/Street Roadster wasn't necessarily pretty, but it sure was quick. Powered by a blown 392 Chrysler, Noyes' roadster easily beat most of the cars it competed against at New England tracks. *Tom Shea Collection*

from his show-quality roadster to go racing at these events, but protégé Paul FitzGerald's primered '32 street roadster was the car to beat, topping 100.

NEHRC eventually found a track at the Sanford, Maine, airport, on a 6,500-foot-long, 200-foot-wide runway. NETA had left about two years earlier, and Orange started operating a year before. The group ran its first race there in July 1955, promoting two races per month for 10 seasons, after which the NEHRC was dissolved, though drag racing continued at Sanford for several more years under the Maine Hot Rod Association.

Drag racing was uppermost in the minds of New England hot rodders in the mid-'50s, and most participants drove their cars to the strip. The most impressive car in the pits was not the fastest. FitzGerald's ever-evolving roadster was a good runner, but its compilation of new ideas reflected his engineering training. In a few years, Fitz's car would pioneer independent front suspension, in two versions. Close friend, and fellow No-Mads member, Pete Seferian had a pretty Deuce roadster, channeled, painstakingly detailed, and powered by an Olds V-8. Like Mudd Sharrigan's car, it had a small Thunderbird-style air scoop with a delicate chrome grille centered on the hood.

There were several memorable street-driven channeled '32 roadsters among the "commuters." Two from southern New Hampshire were Norm Wallace's perennial show winner, built in the traditional style (now owned by Larry Hook), and Norm Kitchen's similar car (owned now by Eddie Bernier, but transformed into a highboy).

To earn the coveted black, red, and gold NEHRC (New England Hot Rod Council) patch, a racer had to top 125 miles per hour in the standing quarter-mile at the Sanford, Maine, strip. As speeds went up, the badge of honor was replaced with a 150-mile-per-hour patch of similar design. *Carl Debien Collection*

(Top Left) This courtesy card left by a Pinions car club member might have been one man's "opinion," but the club's motto clearly defined what the young rodders were striving for: furthering their interest in the "science of auto mechanics." *Ron Carson Collection*

(Top right) Many hot rod clubs' courtesy cards carried the owner's signature on the front or back. Despite the Piston Manglers' rough-and-ready name, the Rutland-based rodders' credence was stated on the card's front: "Safety in Construction—Safety in Operation." *Ron Carson Collection*

(Center right) Dick Pratt, a member of the No-Mads, makes a few trackside repairs to his '34 Ford coupe. Pratt was a founding member of the No-Mads, and is credited with naming the club. *A. B. Shuman*

Fred Steele's dark-purple-with-chrome-everywhere roadster reflected Steele's sense of humor. It was channeled at the suggestion of Ty-Rods confrere Jack Crosby, who had just given his '33 convertible the body-lowering treatment. Crosby helped Steele—using hammers, chisels, and a blowtorch—remove the stock steel floor. With wide whitewalls and a four-carb flathead, it's probably what cartoonist Dave Deal had in mind when he penned his first nose-way-down/tail-way-up, mini-windshield and mini-Deuce shell spoof of an over-the-top hot rod. Steele's was the antithesis of fellow Ty-Rods member Ed Hovagimian's clean, businesslike, and quick street/strip machine. Yet, perhaps because of its outrageous nature, Steele's was the only East Coast car included in the "75 Most Significant 1932

A crowd gathered around Pete Seferian's roadster after the hood top and sides were removed. The Oldsmobile V-8's exhaust resembles that found on many hot rods running Ford flatheads. The chrome side pipes were considered daring for the time, accounting for some of the attention the car always generated. *Tom Shea Collection*

During New England's early days of hot rodding, signup at the drags was a rather simple affair. A few bucks to cover the entry fee allowed you to declare what class your car was eligible to compete in. *Tom Shea Collection*

Ford Hot Rods" chosen to mark the Deuce's seventy-fifth anniversary.

Two 1930 roadsters, Stu Randall's dark blue (Strokers) and Joe "Sonny" Mazza's pale-blue with Chrysler power (Hi-Winder's), represented the Model As. Both are still on the road and well, but Mazza's car is in Oregon.

On the closed-car side, one of the most interesting East Coast hot rods was George Miller's maroon '33 five-window, which he built as a highboy then chopped and channeled after reading in *Hot Rod* how it's done. Its one discordant note was the torpedo tube–like "echo can" exhausts that jutted from the rear of the body on each side of the deck lid. Awarded a trip (courtesy of NETA and the Orange Kiwanis Club) to run at the NHRA Nationals at Great Bend, Kansas, Miller removed the car's headlights and as much weight as he could before losing to a nitro-fueled car in B/Competition class. Despite being eliminated, he was the first New Englander to compete at an NHRA Nationals. In the following years he converted the coupe to a true A/Competition car and found success with a 392 Chrysler Hemi engine.

George Karalekas of the No-Mads owned one of the handsomest, but rarely seen, coupes. A '32 three-window (not chopped, but deeply channeled), its door bottoms were trimmed to clear the chrome side pipes. Cycle fenders, a filled-and-chopped Deuce shell with chromed horizontal tubular grille bars, and solid hood panels with suitcase snaps completed its distinctive look.

In 2006, Fred Steele's purple-and-chrome, chopped-and-channeled roadster was recognized as one of the 75 Most Significant '32 Ford Hot Rods of all time, the only Northeast car to make the list. Originally a highboy, it was channeled with the help of fellow Ty-Rods member Jack Crosby. With this radically raked and chromed car, Steele expressed his extreme approach to hot rods. *A. B. Shuman*

Sammy Packard was a stock car, hydroplane, and midget racer of note. He was also the last surviving member of the group that formed NASCAR at Daytona Beach, Florida's Streamline Hotel in 1947. Most of all, though, Packard was a hot rodder, and he owned two speed shops in Rhode Island. His best-known car was the Olds-powered channeled roadster that crashed on its side during filming for the 1956 B-movie *Hot Rod Girl*.

Today, the Frank Domenichella–channeled '32 five-window is distinguished by the H on its front nerf bar. Fellow Ty-Rods member Kenny Hodges built the coupe in 1951, and Domenichella bought it shortly afterward. Fitted with a three-carb, late-model flathead and '39 floor shift, it was pretty much state-of-the-art at the time. Painted a pale grape color and fitted with four cycle fenders, Domenichella's coupe was clean, straightforward, and devoid of frills. He didn't race it, though he sometimes got stopped for speeding on the way to the races. He sold it in November 2005 when he could no longer get in and out comfortably. After all those years with the coupe, Domenichella said the decision to sell was something he wrestled with. It was last seen in South Carolina.

Kenny Hodges, incidentally, is credited with turning what started as an annual get-together of Ty-Rods members into the Ty-Rods Reunion, one of the top hot rod shows on the East Coast. At first, cars weren't part of the gatherings, but in about 1970, someone posed the notion to include surviving hot rods as well. When perennial club president Fred Steele called Hodges to ask if he'd do that, he got a typically cranky Yankee response: "I'll do it if there are other rods there. But I'm not driving 80 miles up and 80 miles back if mine is the only hot rod there!" Steele

(Left) The Ty-Rods trace their roots to 1952 when a group of young men from Massachusetts met in Carl Carpenter's barn. Originally called the Piston Pushers, they were basically a brash bunch of fun-loving, street-racing punks. Then along came Carroll Sleeper (center in wheelchair), who told the group to shape up or leave. In 1953, the club formed anew, minus the diehard street racers, as the Ty-Rods. Sleeper, a wonderfully apt name for a man who built the unlikeliest fast cars, was a guide and mentor for the group. He was confined to a wheelchair due to a race-related injury. Sleeper's expertise was in building high-performance flathead V-8s. *Carl Carpenter Collection*

(Right) The scales of justice? Hardly. But as drag racing in New England became more sophisticated, the clubs began to keep closer tabs on the cars, making sure they complied with weight rules. Here, members of the New England Timing Association check the weight of a competitor. Those drag slicks, produced by M&H, were another New England product of the time. *Tom Shea Collection*

made sure there were others. That led to more cars the following year, as nonmembers asked if they could bring their old hot rods. Over the years, the show became so successful that the number of entries accepted had to be limited, depending on the location. Wherever it's held, pride of place goes to the old cars.

Recently, New England hot rods built in the 1950s have made a big comeback. Also, other "roots" events have joined the Ty-Rods Reunion in bringing authentic survivor hot rods, both as-is and restored, out of hibernation. That renaissance has also encouraged enthusiasts to build hot rods in the style of those earlier East Coast pioneers.

And, 60 years on, photographers for new, glossier magazines are searching them out for feature stories—that, above all else, is what's changed the most about East Coast hot rodding.

You Have Been Assisted By
A MEMBER OF THE
WORCESTER RAMBLERS
488 PARK AVE.,   WORCESTER, MASS.
An organization of hot rodders, formed into a civic, law-abiding, constructive group, dedicated to..........
"SAFE AND SANE DRIVING ON THE HIGHWAY."
Member's Name _Cly Robertson_

Club members carried courtesy cards, like this one from the Worcester Ramblers, and handed them out to people they assisted along the road. It was a good public relations gesture that helped elevate hot rodders' reputations from road warriors to road knights. *Ron Carson Collection*

CHAPTER 7

Just knocking around. Tommy Gill shows friend Don Ferrara, sitting on the front wheel, his Merc-powered Model T roadster set on 1932 rails. The photo was taken March 28, 1946. *Don Ferrara Collection*

HOT ROD HERITAGE

Evolution, not revolution, fuels the fire

By Mark A. Morton

THE FOUNDING OF *HOT RODDING* inevitably paralleled the development of the automobile. Hot rodding started spontaneously, as Henry Ford and other pioneers of the auto industry hopped up race cars to demonstrate the reliability and exceptional performance of their tin progeny. The credence "Win on Sunday to sell on Monday" held true then, as it does today.

Consequently, hot rodding as we know it more or less evolved from the racetrack to the street. Any man might actually try his hand at performance tweaks, miming the racers; the aesthetic thing also may have emulated those racers, or more exclusive models seen on the street and in magazines of the day. Whatever the case, the individual could have his way with an automobile, setting himself and his car apart from the boring masses.

Some of us look to the experience and history of those stalwart rodders of the 1920s and 1930s, and to the performance innovators (Harry Miller, Ed Winfield, George Riley, et al) for inspiration and to sate our ravenous appetite for the history of this hobby, sport, pastime, or whatever you want to call it that has us wound so tight. The most obvious starting point, however, at least to newcomers, is the postwar period. It has been chronicled—almost ad infinitum—such that people with even the most newfound interest in hot rodding can recite facts, figures, and nomenclature of the postwar era without knowing much about the prewar period.

This could be a scene from any year, any place. The Fulkerson-Solomon team has their Cragar-Ford engine disassembled on the dry lake bed. The team ran as members of the Hollywood Auto Club during 1942 and managed 112 miles per hour at this September meet. *Julian Doty Collection*

Don Ferrara's 1929 Ford roadster in the build stage. The date is December 26, 1943, so progress was probably impeded by the war effort. He got the car for free, and years later it would grace the covers of *Hot Rod* and *Hop Up* magazines. *Don Ferrara Collection*

History is taught in school as a necessary starting reference point for children to begin to understand what caused mankind to get where we are politically, socially, economically, and otherwise. Folks become enchanted with interactions of the individuals who participated in history, and derive pleasure from research, learning, understanding, and forming opinions about what drove certain people to behave as they did. You can research, develop your own impressions and visions of an era, and "go back" for a clearer understanding.

Civil War reenactment comes to mind. What better way to understand the War Between the States and appreciate our predecessors who fought in it than to act out and create our own version? Reenactments serve as homage to our predecessors and fulfill a need to see nonexistent videos of the events, thus keeping the history topical while paying respects.

Vintage motorsports, in this case hot rodding, serves the same purpose for automotive enthusiasts. We *go back* every time we light the motor on that hot rod; it's a magic carpet ride into automotive history, such that we can seek our own journey down the idyllic two-lane—the road that confesses no modern attributes, no connection with the calendar of today.

Such, too, is the experience in the garage, shop, or barn; that's where we lay hands on tools and hardware, same as those icons Winfield, Alex Xydias, Ed Iskenderian, and thousands of others, most of whose names we don't even know. Some of us must do this to fulfill our self-imposed

The streets of Los Angeles in the 1940s seemed broad and were free of the heavy traffic that hinders drivers today. This photo shows Don Ferrara's roadster driven by his buddy Moe Ogston. The date is January 20, 1946. *Don Ferrara Collection*

A youthful Don Ferrara (left), joined by his friend Al Barns, takes a time out alongside his A-V8 roadster on 98th Street in Los Angeles between Figueroa and Broadway. The location is now a freeway off-ramp. Barns later gained fame with his high-performance oil pumps. *Don Ferrara Collection*

indentured obligation to the hobby; we feel apprenticed to the honor of the people so nobly chronicled by The American Hot Rod Foundation. It's ritual. Cathartic. We just dig hot rods.

Classics, vintage sports cars, antique trucks, custom cars, and all the rest are celebrated elsewhere every day, too, while their own student/practitioners pursue the obsession to whatever degree scratches the itch. Some of us are *pretty* itchy, too.

But how'd we get right *here*, where we are now?

In hot rodding, evolution is a given. Performance drives our rod population, and most of that performance is fed by innovation and invention as technology advances; manufacturers and racers (factory-backed, as well as independent teams and in-the-barn grassroots ventures) continually have found new ways to squeeze horsepower out of their engines and to improve handling.

Aesthetics followed as the need to be different—even iconoclastic—bred innovation. Postwar hot rods developed the trademark look that remains with us today. The social phenomenon of *cool* was part of that, and it's with us today. Specifically, the icon of the traditional hot rod is deemed to be the postwar roadster, whether in primer or paint; it had, and has, that *look* with which we are cozily familiar. Styling treatments were defined and almost rhetorical: dropped axle, big/little tires and wheels, chopped top or windshield posts laid back, filled radiator shell, shaved handles. Ford teardrop taillights or '41 Chev lights. Sometimes the body was channeled over the frame; some fellas with enough scratch and know-how would get the rear ends low, too.

In every case, the *look* had been defined. It was then, and it is now.

Randy Shinn's 1927 T roadster at El Mirage Dry Lake on August 18, 1946—the day he ran 124.48 miles per hour. Randy was a member of the Road Runners, and his consistent—and fast—performances that year earned him SCTA co-champion honors. *Don Ferrara Collection*

The Tom Beatty and Barney Navarro entry is seen at the lakes on April 24–25, 1948. Car No. 240 had a supercharged Ford flathead engine. No time was recorded, so can we assume the engine blew up? One of the first teams to explore the use of supercharging, they encountered many setbacks like this. *Don Ferrara Collection*

When World War II ended, hot rodders had a lot of catching up to do at the dry lakes. Behind this pristine 1940 Ford Deluxe Coupe waits a gaggle of roadsters ready to do battle on the dry lake.

Evolution was subtle at first. While the character of that traditional hot rod was maintained, there was departure resulting from the build process. Evolution (side-stepped by traditional guys) is driven by aspirations of enhanced performance, and in some measure, by product manufacturers who have a vested interest in changing products, creating trends, and exploiting markets for next, newest, best. Traditional consumers, though, have enjoyed a kind of stasis that realizes certain unavoidable evolution but resists dramatic change as departing from the soul of the endeavor. They won't dignify change for change's sake, or dare to appear trendy.

The course of change is traceable, generally, by the decades. A hot rod built in the 1940s has a different look from one built in, say, the 1970s.

In the 1950s, many former lakes race cars tested their mettle at the drag strip and became largely single-purpose cars rather than the commuters with stripped fenders and headlights we see in 1940s-era dry lakes pictures. Other hot rods migrated to the street. They were painted, plated, trimmed, and rimmed for the occasion. Hubcaps. Whitewalls. Custom stitchwork. And *chrome*. A fragmentation of the community was taking place—evolving.

The *street rod* was born. Hot rod evolution was defined yet again.

Much of this actualization was magazine-driven as the East and West coasts (and parts of the Heartland) compared notes and styles with no innovation missed by enthusiasts in any part of the country. Names outside of racing and performance products began to percolate to the front of the rodders' consciousness. In the late 1950s, the L.A. Roadsters formed to feature beautifully turned-out rods (all roadsters, as the club's name suggests) that went on . . . *rod runs*. Hot rod (some insisted on the label *street* rod) magazines prospered, and there became a social acceptance of sorts credited in no small measure to the National Hot Rod Association, founded in 1951. They went drag racing, mostly, but we all tuned in, be it street or strip. Or *show*.

In the early 1960s, the street phenomenon was slowing down, and another generation that had been too young to participate in the 1940s and 1950s—but which had taken notice—blossomed. By the end of the decade they had brought *street* back into the equation. See, organized drag

A bird's-eye view of the starting line at El Mirage Dry Lake for the April 24–25, 1948, SCTA meet. Three staging lanes, complete with timing lights, made for some rapid-fire racing. No. 522 is the Class D Roadster belonging to Sidewinders member R. L. Reed. It used a 1932 Cadillac V-12 with a Winfield cam for power. Reed clicked the clocks at 114.67 miles per hour in his channeled '32 Ford. Initially, the SCTA allowed only road-sters, but eventually expanded its program to include closed-top cars. *Don Ferrara Collection*

racing—for all the good it has done and is doing—was an early death sentence for *street* hot rods. By the time I came up in the 1960s, hot rods were nearly off the street in my 'hood. If not for the L.A. Roadsters and, later, the Early Times car club, we'd have had no examples to look back on. The Early Times (I cite them for their proximity to my birthright in Southern California) symbolized the new group of hot rodders. Feverish detail began to show—American Racing Torq Thrusts, Cragar five-spokes, and Skylark wires, not to mention a surge in aftermarket products, highlighted the era. To be sure, street was still sepa-rate from the strip and lakes. They didn't necessarily oppose each other, but rather formed separate communities with overlapping mutual interests.

The National Street Rod Association's (NSRA) Nationals, L.A. Roadsters, Early Times, and fledging parts companies like Pete & Jake's proved influential in the return to the street. Hot rods were going to be hot rods—or street rods (more later)—and not just drag racers. Two-tone paint schemes with candy colors and lace graphics and webbing inlays (ugh!) were styling fads that distinguish the 1970s from all other eras in hot rod-ding's colorful history.

Touring in hot rods was celebrated in the magazines, influencing guys to build depend-able cars, for which good hardware was required. The numbers of those guys so inclined—and their resultant demand for the parts and ability to *pay* for them—boosted the street rod aftermarket industry, and the game was on.

The era defined itself with resto-rods, family-oriented events, the NSRA, cast-iron Powerglide transmissions, and bud vases tacked inside the interiors. Big tires bulged outside the fenders, and men wore white belts and shoes and double-knit pants. The baby boomers were growing up and having families, and their careers provided them with discretionary income that allowed street rod projects. A few, though, stubbornly cleaved to traditional hot rod styling and tricks, a style that—to their credit—would resuscitate almost 20 years later as *trend*. Throughout, there remained a vestige of traditional hot rodding, but it wasn't current or fashionable. Those cats were definitely under the radar.

So, the guys were growing up. They raised their families, pursued their careers, and some actually got empty-nested ahead of the rest of us!

Then that constant—change—once again mobilized, and billet and smoothies entered the mainstream as the success (excess) of the next decade fostered the next step for the boomers. The 1980s affected our car world just as they affected all areas of society. Yuppies came to the hot rod party; their projects were still hot rods, morphed into their modern vision of self-expression. Tradition lived on, though, if inauspiciously. The cars' visual reference was still 1920s, '30s, and '40s cars, modified to suit, so the thread—that pedigree—remained a quiet constant. Style, trends, and other opportunities took some participants in other directions—muscle cars were old enough to be restored by then, for example—allowing hot rods to become an evolved mutation of their own species.

An exciting mainstreaming took place for many hot rod enthusiasts during this time. Their cars followed a pattern—a mold—that few seemed able to break loose from. The few guys, however, stubbornly cleaved to traditional style and parts seemed to be an obscure minority. Modern hot rods were more palatable to the mainstream, we guess, and high-profile magazines outside the rod world featured "$100,000 street rod" articles. Builders such as Boyd Coddington drew lots of attention to the sport/hobby/business of street rodding, and several companies went public. Some made it and some didn't. The billet and smoothie trend commanded the 1980s, but the inevitable—change—was again afoot.

In the '90s we saw the enthusiast population increase, and it was here that the fork in the road was paved. Modern hot rods and phantom rods (which pay sometimes-reluctant respects to the pedigree in that they are—or are supposed to look like—pre-'49 cars) were the cover darlings of the mainstream, but the other fork (maybe it was a dirt road after all!) was heading to traditional town. Here, a retro movement celebrated the roots. Traditional styles were seen to have charm and challenge in an archeological and anthropological way. The 1940s and 1950s had cachet. Nostalgia was becoming fashionable, but not in a Richie Cunningham way. Instead, it had to do with heritage. *Tradition* was in style.

Don Montgomery's books had much to do with this revelation of our heritage, and many of us experienced solace in the simplicity and heart of the early cars and the experiences of the car owners and builders. Retro got more and more popular, thanks to an adjunct that became known as the "rat rod" movement. The two overlapped much of the time, but were markedly different via the former's less stylized aesthetic.

There had always been an axiom that a car had to be pre-'49 to be a hot rod. You can stretch that cutoff date to make the attendance larger at rod runs, and even the most evolved phantom cars kinda look pre-'49, but the fact is that hot rods *are* pre-'49. And in all of this

Hot rodding has always been a labor of love. Indeed, the facilities at the dry lakes haven't changed much over the years. The pit area, especially, remains the same as it was when this photo was taken in the late 1940s. About all a guy could really count on was that the lake bed's alkaline dust would get into the car's every nook and cranny.

varied culture, the common thread, the touchstone, is the traditional hot rod. It's the look, the soul of the hot rod being.

And is it really the tale of the baby boom generation after all? It might well be, but it's certainly also about those who raised the boomers, and we should also include those the boomers *raised*. Our fathers and grandfathers provided us with a societal circumstance that would avail recreational opportunity unlike any group before us. Until the twentieth century, subsistence living had been the goal, and *we* were set up so that we could choose among things as silly as jumping out of airplanes or—yes—conspicuously consuming fossil fuel to wile away our surplus time and discretionary loot. Not bad. The economic well-being of our population and our quality of life can be distilled by looking at our motorsport population from the '30s to present. Amid that growing excess, our guys made the choice to indulge in personal ideals of perfection via old-car performance and appearance. Thus, the above and the prior chapters, right?

The problem may be that we have balled it all up, and those who follow may not have the same options. The verdict is not in. Society as a whole hasn't been much on our (motorsport) side all along, anyway, has it? The thing that nips us in our offbeat bud may be something as basic as fuel conservation.

Today, there's an ecumenical nature to motorsport—car nuts feel akin to one another. Oh, sure, there are snobs who look askance at hot rods, and there are some factions that we,

too, dismiss as silly. And there are even snob-rodders with the elitist views that their slice of the rodding pie is more meaningful than another guy's. It's the human condition, boys. Rat rods, retro-rods, Roth rods—call 'em whatever the favored term is this month—are the new blood, though. Those hot rod niches hearken to history and then some, and no doubt their circle of taste overlaps considerably with the traditional guys.

In a demographic dissection of the folks indulging in all this foolishness (the hot rod culture), we find three human generations in the species: Greasers, Graybeards, and Galoots. You know 'em.

Swarming their own styles, Greasers can't "get" modern hot rods. Rat/Roth rods are the blank canvas of this younger set, and although there is the odd Galoot or Graybeard among 'em, they are the exception.

Graybeards might go either way, splitting themselves mostly between billet and traditional. Galoots, who favor stock or traditional, just don't understand rat rods.

In a graphic illustration we can visualize the three circles representing those groups, and align them over a chart of rodding evolution: Modern Hot Rods, Traditional Hot Rods, and Rat/Roth rods. At the top sits the current, most evolved form of the genre: Modern Hot Rods. They draw almost no interest from Greasers and little from Galoots, remaining the domain of Graybeards, who constitute the center of the demographic.

Aficionados from the Greaser set cleave somewhat to the Traditional group, in which Graybeards major. Galoots split their time between Traditional rods and stockers.

But Traditional rods, in the center, where the generation circles overlap and become almost concentric at moments, is the prime area where a certain pedigree style or concept is pursued and consumed by a communal blend of all three generations.

Generally the beat of Graybeards, but shared with all, here's the real ecumenical, universal experience in rodding. The truth of traditional hot rods is that they nourish the passions of all generations. Here, we all worship at the same Temple of Gow, in an unlikely reunion of all age groups.

Traditionalists tend to enjoy a conciliatory interchange with restorers, too. Contrary to the rhetorical notion that stocker guys hate hot rodders, the (usually) older stocker guys are much the same age as Galoots and Graybeards. (We have, in fact, commented that stockers are closer to our truth than are Modern Hot Rods.) A traditional rodder is more likely to covet, study, or enjoy a stocker than a conventional modern street rod. Most Traditional rodders are committed more to core values than to evolution.

Neither has growing older seemed to change the aesthetic. The ethic of traditionalists is fairly constant as they dig deeper into the history and biographies of rodding's elders, taking the other two generations along with them on a hot rod bacchanal back to *the day*. The semantic dicing that takes place over *street rod* and *hot rod* serves a purpose, if only to establish a definition for communication in this era. A *street rod* is the evolved, morphed, modernized result of a few dozen years of the hot rod chronology. The *hot rod* is not.

The *hot rod* is rather more base, suffering from the invisible ceiling we place on the aesthetics, stubbornly settling for performance mods available only up to a certain time (i.e., the common boast "nothing manufactured after 1949 will be found on this roadster"). Whether it is the will to go back to a simpler time or the thrill of engaging the hobby "just like the founders did," truth (we call it *veritas*) is in tradition. Fashion cycles on and on, and this hot rod faction is the style segment that can claim all three (now redundant) generations: Greasers, Graybeards, and Galoots.

When all is said and done, what remains is the pedigree, the traditional style. It's the unifying element that finds common purpose in the hot rodders' efforts, whether they are Modern, Traditional, or Rat/Roth. The premise has always been to modify pre-'49 cars. Like it or not, Fords are/were the brand of choice, owing a lot to Henry's clever insistence that parts might not have to be remade or redesigned each year, resulting in a handy interchangeability, not to mention that Henry's workers made scads of 'em. So, you made them hotter, you made them look better (or at least different), and you had yourself a hot rod. The hobby can't evolve completely away from that early concept or it will no longer be hot rodding. So, traditional hot rods remain the touchstone, ground zero. You start from here, do your mischief to personalize it, give it your own interpretation. Express your art and craft. If you start somewhere farther down the evolutionary chain, and some do, well, then you ain't one of us.

We're left with the truth that *tradition* is the base of this artistic, mechanical celebration that we call hot rodding. It is for the obsessed. It is for those who would have an outlet for expression and it is for the *cool*. Don't forget that last one. The axiom? Hot Rods are Cool, meaning that hot rodders—by rank association—are, too.

Just leave the bud vases out of the equation, okay?

After a long day at the local Southern California dry lake, Joe Staytan and Ed Madsen head back to the town of Lancaster. This small community was the closest point of civilization for the racers who competed at the nearby dry lakes, including Muroc, El Mirage, Harper, and Rosamond. *Nordskog Family Collection*

Acknowledgments

Without the combined efforts of various individuals, a book of this magnitude would take forever to complete. As the field editor for *Hot Rod Roots*, I'm indebted to key players who helped make this book a reality, among them, Motorbooks' Dennis Pernu, whose word skills assisted me in making this anthology a smooth read.

In turn, I'd like to thank Alex Xydias for bridging the generation gap so that seven "young" writers could give deeper meaning to their respective chapters. Those writers are Pat Ganahl, Robert Genat, Ken Gross, Mark Morton, Greg Sharp, A. B. Shuman, and me. Thank you all for your words about a subject that's obviously very dear to each of you.

On behalf of this book's writers, I thank The American Hot Rod Foundation for the opportunity to participate in this project. Led by Steve Memishian, the foundation has created a permanent home for hot rodding's heritage. Foundation personnel such as Henry Astor and R. Ellen Avellino, along with the advisory board, have enabled the AHRF to flourish. I would be remiss, too, not to mention the long hours spent by Jim Miller, the foundation's archivist, preserving in digital format the thousands of old photographs that have been donated for posterity. Jim's careful cataloging—not to mention his thorough researching, annotating, and captioning—was responsible for many of the photographs you've enjoyed in this book. And a special thanks, again, to A. B. Shuman for gathering photos from the "Right Coast" to include in his chapter about the early days of hot rodding east of the Mississippi.

On a personal note, I'd like to dig deep into my past as a hot rod journalist and thank a few key players who helped me find my allotted place in this profession. First, to LeRoi "Tex" Smith, who, as editorial director at *Street Rodder*, gave me my first staff-writer job back in 1971. Ditto to that magazine's first publisher, the late Tom McMullen, along with Jim Clark and Rich Bean (my first editors).

Finally, thank you to my wife, Donna, and two sons, Kyle and Chris, for their support, and to the Big Publisher who gave me the gift of writing (which has enabled me to *not* have to work a day in my entire adult life). Writing is a pleasure. Thanks, Big Guy.

Dain Gingerelli
Mission Viejo, California
May 2007

About the Writers

Alex Xydias is a name synonymous with So-Cal Speed Shop and, indeed, the sport of hot rodding. In 1946, after his discharge from the army, Alex opened So-Cal Speed Shop. While the shop initially struggled to make a decent turnover, the So-Cal racing team's success on the dry lakes, particularly with the So-Cal belly tank, became legendary. Alex then partnered with hot rod pioneer Dean Batchelor to campaign the So-Cal streamliner, and together they broke every record in their class. Running an Edelbrock-equipped V8-60 built by Bobby Meeks, the car turned 152 miles per hour; then, with a Mercury V-8, it turned 210 at Bonneville, far outpacing the competition. The So-Cal team continued to build cars that would shatter most existing records at the lakes and on the drag strips. Now restored to its former glory, the So-Cal belly tank is one of the most famous hot rods ever.

Steve Memishian is a former mechanical engineer, management consultant, and motion-picture executive who found his way to Wall Street and now manages money at DSM Capital Partners in New York. Steve sketched Deuce coupes and roadsters on his high school notebooks but doesn't remember seeing any in Winchester, Massachusetts, in the 1950s and '60s. When he finally got into hot rodding much later in life, he was shocked to find that no one had committed themselves to the purpose of preserving and promoting the histories of hot rodding's pioneers. That realization led Steve, his wife, Carol, and his brother, Jack, to found The American Hot Rod Foundation.

Robert Genat has an intimate understanding of automobiles, having worked at Ford Motor Company for 13 years as a body designer. In 1993, he left the corporate world to shoot photos and write full-time. As of this publication, he has authored more than 30 books and 100 magazine articles. In 2000, Robert was selected for an International Automotive Media Award for his book *The American Car Dealership*. He has been honored three times for his writing by The American Auto Racing Writers & Broadcasters Association. In 2001, his *Funny Cars* was selected as one of AARWBA's top auto racing books; in 2002, Robert's *American Drag Racing* was selected by AARWBA as the year's best book on auto racing.

Pat Ganahl is a native Southern Californian and a veteran of the hot rod and custom scenes as a writer, photographer, archivist, and participant. He is the former editor of *Hot Rod*, *Rod & Custom*, *Street Rodder*, and *The Rodder's Journal*, as well as a contributor to several other publications in the United States and abroad. He has also written 10 books in the field, ranging from technical subjects to works on Von Dutch, Ed "Big Daddy" Roth, and the American custom car. Current projects in his garage include a Cad-powered '32 Ford roadster and the Ike Iacono 12-port GMC vintage dragster.

Greg Sharp has been referred to in the hot rod press as "the rod and custom trivia king" (*Rod & Custom*) and "one of the most knowledgeable hot rod historians on the planet" (*Goodguys Gazette*). He's participated in all forms of hot rodding, from racing at Bonneville to judging custom car shows nationwide. He's best known for the hundreds of magazine articles he's written, ranging from a history of America's Most Beautiful Roadster to pieces on motorsport, hot rod, and custom personalities from A. J. Foyt to George Barris. He serves as curator of the Wally Parks NHRA Motorsports Museum in Pomona, California, and is a member of the Grand National Roadster Show Hall of Fame and the Dry Lakes Racing Hall of Fame.

Dain Gingerelli has been writing about cars and motorcycles since 1970. He earned a degree in communications at California State University, Fullerton, and road-raced motorcycles and cars for 13 years, in the course winning four amateur-class championships and four FIM world endurance speed records. Dain was associate editor for *Street Rodder*'s premier issue in 1972, and his byline and photo credits have appeared on countless motorcycle and automotive magazine articles. Additionally, he has authored six hot rod books, most recently *The Cars of Overhaulin'* (Motorbooks, 2007). He currently lives in Mission Viejo, California, with his wife and two sons. Dain's daily driver is a 1964 Chevy II Nova two-door. "It's all original," says Dain, "but I'm slowly changing that."

Ken Gross has been an automotive writer for more than 30 years. Formerly the director of the Petersen Automotive Museum, he writes frequently for *Street Rodder*, *The Rodder's Journal*, *Hop Up*, and *Old Cars Weekly*. His articles on hot rods have also appeared in *Road & Track*, *Car Collector*, *Mobilia*, *Octane*, and *The Robb Report*. Ken writes with a particular passion that's due to his significant personal involvement in the hobby: his hot rods have been the subject of many magazine articles by other authors, and his collection of manifolds and other period hot rod parts is a source of great pleasure to him. Ken travels constantly and can often be found prowling the swap meets of car shows across the country.

A. B. Shuman discovered hot rodding in the mid-'50s as a teen in Sharon, Massachusetts. He soon began writing about it in the school and town papers, and nationally, in *Drag News*, while racing in his brother Bernie's '32 roadster. After receiving a degree in mechanical engineering, he became a naval aviator, but still wrote for the weekly *Drag World*. After his navy service, he was hired by *Car Craft* and later served as editor of *Hot Rod* and executive editor of *Motor Trend*. He returned to the East Coast in 1972, joining Mercedes-Benz and becoming public relations director in 1991. In 1995, A. B. purchased a flathead-powered track T that soon led him to begin work with his brother on the 1999 book *Cool Cars, Square Roll Bars* about '50s hot rodding in New England. Still active in New England hot rodding events, A. B. currently drives a blown flathead-powered altered '23 T roadster.

Mark Morton fell in love with hot rodding early. As soon as his feet could touch the pedals, he was "borrowing" his dad's custom '38 Ford pickup. After a modicum of business success, Mark was finally able to build up a serious collection of rods and customs, including a '29 roadster, a '65 Riviera, and the '33 Lincoln KB Judkins Coupe originally owned by G. Henry Stetson. In 1992 Mark bought *Hop Up* magazine and has maintained its integrity and informational value for all hot rod enthusiasts. Following the success of *Hop Up*, Mark established www.hopupmag.com. His editorials there are a special treat.

Index